THE LIBRARY OF TRADITIONAL WISDOM

The Library of Traditional Wisdom has as its aim to present a series of works founded on Tradition, this term being defined as the transmission, over time, of permanent and universal truths, whose written sources are the revealed Scriptures as well as the writings of the great spiritual masters.

This series is thus dedicated to the *Sophia Perennis* or *Religio Perennis* which is the timeless metaphysical truth underlying the diverse religions, together with its essential methodological consequences.

It is in the light of the *Sophia Perennis,* which views every religion "from within," that may be found the keys of an adequate understanding which, joined to the sense of the sacred, alone can safeguard the irreplaceable values and genuine spiritual possibilities of the great religions.

The Transfiguration of Man

Frithjof Schuon

WORLD WISDOM BOOKS, INC.

© 1995 by Frithjof Schuon

Translated from the French

Published in French as
La Transfiguration de l'Homme
Editions Maisonneuve Larose, Paris, 1995

Library of Congress Cataloging-in-Publication Data

Schuon, Frithjof, 1907-
  [Transfiguration de l'Homme. English]
  The Transfiguration of Man / Frithjof Schuon
      p. cm.
  Includes bibliographical references.
  ISBN 0-941532-19-4 (pbk. : alk. paper)
  1. Man. 2. Spiritual life. I. Title.
BD450.S38213   1995
248.4--dc20   95-10140

The cover photo is a carving of the Chinese *yin-yang*,
symbol of cosmic and universal polarity.

Printed on acid-free paper in The United States of America

For information address World Wisdom Books, Inc.
P. O. Box 2682, Bloomington, Indiana 47402-2682

Table of Contents

Foreword

The image of man presented to us by modern psychology is not only fragmentary, it is pitiable. In reality, man is as if suspended between animality and divinity; now modern thought — be it philosophical or scientific — admits only animality, practically speaking.

We wish, on the contrary, to correct and perfect the image of man by insisting on his divinity; not that we wish to make a god of him, *quod absit*; we intend simply to take account of his true nature, which transcends the earthly, and lacking which he would have no reason for being.

It is this that we believe we can call — in a symbolist language — the "transfiguration of man."

Part One

Thought, Art and Work

Thought: Light and Perversion

It should be possible to restore to the word "philosophy" its original meaning: philosophy — the "love of wisdom" — is the science of all the fundamental principles; this science operates with intuition, which "perceives," and not with reason alone, which "concludes." Subjectively speaking, the essence of philosophy is certitude; for the moderns, on the contrary, the essence of philosophy is doubt: philosophy is supposed to reason without any premise *(voraussetzungsloses Denken)*, as if this condition were not itself a preconceived idea; this is the classical contradiction of all relativism. Everything is doubted except for doubt.[1]

The solution to the problem of knowledge — if there is a problem — could not possibly be this intellectual suicide that is the promotion of doubt; on the contrary, it lies in having recourse to a source of certitude that transcends the mental mechanism, and this source — the only one there is — is the pure Intellect, or Intelligence as such. The so-called century of "enlightenment" did not suspect its existence; for the Encyclopedists, all that the Intellect had offered — from Pythagoras to the Scholastics — was merely naive dogmatism, even "obscurantism." Quite paradoxically, the cult of reason ended in that sub-rationalism — or

---

1. For Kant, intellectual intuition — of which he does not understand the first word — is a fraudulent manipulation *(Erschleichung),* which throws a moral discredit onto all authentic intellectuality.

3

"esoterism of stupidity" — that is existentialism in all its forms; it is to illusorily replace intelligence with "existence."

Some have believed it is possible to replace the premise of thought by the arbitrary, empirical and altogether subjective element that is the "personality" of the thinker, which amounts to the very destruction of the notion of truth; one may as well renounce all philosophy. The more thought wishes to be "concrete," the more it is perverse; this began with empiricism, the first step towards the dismantling of the spirit; originality is sought, and perish the truth.[2]

It is the sophists, with Protagoras at their head, who are the true precursors of modern thought; they are the "thinkers" properly so called, in the sense that they limited themselves to reasoning and were hardly concerned with "perceiving" and taking into account that which "is." And it is a mistake to see in Socrates, Plato and Aristotle the fathers of rationalism, or even of modern thought generally; no doubt they reasoned — Shankara and Ramanuja did so as well — but they never said that reasoning is the alpha and omega of intelligence and of truth, nor a fortiori that our experiences or our tastes determine thought and have priority over intellectual intuition and logic, *quod absit*.

On the whole, modern philosophy is the codification of an acquired infirmity; the intellectual atrophy of man marked by the "fall" entails a hypertrophy of practical intelligence, whence in the final analysis the explosion of the physical sciences and the appearance of pseudo-sciences such as psychology and sociology.[3]

2. It is not of philosophy, but of "misosophy" that one ought to speak here. This term has been rightly applied to the paranoid ideologues of the nineteenth century, and the least one can say is that it has not lost any of its applicability.

3. In the nineteenth century, the desire to reconcile faith and reason, or the religious spirit and science, appeared in the form of occultism: a

Be that as it may, it has to be acknowledged that rationalism benefits from extenuating circumstances in the face of religion, to the extent that rationalism becomes the mouthpiece of legitimate needs for causality raised by certain dogmas, at least when these are taken literally, as theology demands.[4] In an altogether general way, it goes without saying that a rationalist can be right on the level of observations and experiences; man is not a closed system, although he can try to be so.

But even aside from any question of rationalism and dogmatism, one cannot begrudge anyone for being scandalized by the stupidities and the crimes perpetrated in the name of religion, or even simply by the antinomies between the different creeds; however, since horrors are assuredly not the appanage of religion — the preachers of the "goddess reason" furnish the proof of this — it is necessary to confine ourselves to the observation that excesses and abuses are a part of human nature. If it is absurd and shocking that crimes claim the authority of the Holy Spirit, it is no less illogical and scandalous that they take place in the shadow of an ideal of rationality and justice.

It is necessary to take into account here the corrupting magic of error, whether the framework be religious or worldly; this magic can even affect superior men; *errare humanum est.* No doubt, "the end justifies the means"; but on condition that the means not villify the end!

Among other things, what characterizes the rationalist spirit, is a retrospective, not prospective critical sense; the psychosis of "civilization" and of "progress" attest to this to repletion. Clearly, the critical sense is in itself a good that is

hybrid phenomenon that despite its phantasmagoria had some merits, if only by its opposition to materialism and confessional superficiality.

4. There were "voices of wisdom" — not sceptical, but positive and constructive — on the side of the believers themselves, within the framework of Scholasticism and that of the Renaissance; also within that of the Reformation, with the old theosophers for example.

indispensable, but it requires a spiritual context that justifies it and gives it the right proportion.

It is not surprising that the aesthetics of the rationalists admits only the art of classical Antiquity, which in fact inspired the Renaissance, then the world of the Encyclopedists of the French Revolution and, to a great extent, the entire nineteenth century. Now this art — which, by the way, Plato did not appreciate — strikes one by its combination of rationality and sensual passion: its architecture has something cold and poor about it — spiritually speaking — while its sculpture is totally lacking in metaphysical transparency and thereby in contemplative depth.[5] It is all that inveterately cerebral men could desire.

A rationalist can be right — man not being a closed system — as we have said above. In modern philosophy, valid insights can in fact be met with, notwithstanding that their general context compromises and weakens them. Thus the "categorical imperative" does not mean much on the part of a thinker who denies metaphysics and with it the transcendent causes of moral principles, and who is unaware that intrinsic morality is above all our conformity to the nature of Being.

*

* *

As regards the impasses of theology — to which unbelievers have the right to be sensitive — we must have recourse to metaphysics in order to elucidate the basis of the problem. The apparent "absurdities" that certain formulations imply are explained above all by the voluntarist and simplifying tendency inherent in monotheistic piety, whence a priori the reduction of the supreme mysteries — pertaining

---

5. In Greek art there are two errors or two limitations: the architecture expresses reasoning man inasmuch as he intends to victoriously oppose himself to virgin Nature; the sculpture replaces the miracle of profound beauty and life by a more or less superficial beauty and by marble.

to the suprapersonal Divine Principle — to the personal Divine Principle. This is the distinction between Beyond-Being and Being, or between the "Godhead" and "God" *(Gottheit* and *Gott)* in Eckhartian terms; or again, in Vedantic terms: between the "supreme" *Brahma (Para-Brahma)* and the "non-supreme" *Brahma, (Apara-Brahma).* Now in Semitic monotheist theology, the personal God is not conceived as the projection of the pure Absolute; on the contrary, the pure Absolute is considered — to the extent that there is presentiment of It — as the Essence of this already relative Absolute that is the personal God, Who always is accentuated and Who occupies the center and the summit. As a result, there are serious difficulties from the standpoint of the logic of things, but which are "unperceived" from the standpoint of the fear and love of God: thus, All-Possibility and Omnipotence pertain in reality to Beyond-Being; they do not pertain to Being except through participation and in a relative and unilateral fashion, which exonerates the Principle-Being from a certain cosmological "responsibility."

In speaking above of apparent "absurdities," we had in view above all the idea of a God at once infinitely powerful and infinitely good Who creates a world filled with imperfections and calamities, including an eternal hell. Only metaphysics can resolve these enigmas which faith imposes upon the believer, and which he accepts because he accepts God; not out of naivety, but thanks to a certain instinct for the essential and for the supernatural. It is precisely the loss of this instinct that allowed rationalism to flower and spread; piety having weakened, impiety was able to assert itself. And if on the one hand the world of faith unquestionably comprises naivety, on the other hand the world of reason totally lacks intellectual and spiritual intuition, which is much more serious; it is the loss of the sacred and the death of the spirit.

Rather than arguing vainly over what God "wills" or "does not will," theologians readily reply, and rightly so, with an estoppel: who art thou, man, to wish to fathom the reasons of thy Creator? God is incomprehensible, and incomprehensible are His decrees; which, from the standpoint of earthly *māyā*, is the strict truth and the only truth that the humanity to which the religious Message is addressed is capable of fruitfully assimilating. An assimilation more moral than intellectual: Platonism cannot be preached to sinners in danger of perdition, for whom reality is the world "such as it is."

*

* *

As can be seen from what we have said, our intention is not to insinuate that religion should be other than what it is. The religions have had no choice: the rift, in the average man of the "iron age," between the Intellect and an extroverted and superficial intelligence, has obliged them to treat adults like children on pain of psychological, moral and social inefficacy. The profane ideologies on the contrary treat as adults men rendered almost irresponsible by their passions and their illusions, which means that they incite them to play with fire; one sees only too well the sinister results of this in our age. In religious exoterisms, efficacy at times takes the place of truth, and rightly so, given the nature of the men to whom they are addressed. In other words: for the voluntaristic and moralistic theologian, that is true which will yield a good result; for the born metaphysician, on the contrary, that is efficacious which is true; "there is no right superior to that of the Truth." But not everyone is a "pneumatic," and it is necessary to give societies an equilibrium and to save souls as one can.

On the one hand, it is obvious that gnosis has the right to exist; on the other, it is also quite clear that the theologians take a dim view of it. To begin with, the partisans of "faith" reduce intelligence to reason alone, and then, they accuse intelligence of "intellectual pride" — a contradiction in terms — the moment that it follows the demands of its own nature. It is the reverse of what the rationalists do, who reproach gnosis for replacing intelligence by a gratuitous dogmatism and an irrational mysticism.

But the rationalists and the fideists are not the only adversaries of the *Sophia Perennis:* another opponent — somewhat unexpected — is what we could term "realizationism" or "ecstatism": namely the mystical prejudice — rather widespread in India — which has it that only "realization" or "states" count in spirituality. The partisans of this opinion oppose "concrete realization" to "vain thought" and they too easily imagine that with ecstasy all is won; they forget that without the doctrines — beginning with the Vedanta! — they would not even exist; and it also happens that they forget that a subjective realization — founded on the idea of the immanent "Self" — greatly has need of the objective element that is the Grace of the personal God, without forgetting the concurrence of Tradition.

We must mention here the existence of false masters who, as inheritors of occultism and inspired by "realizationism" and psychoanalysis, contrive to invent implausible infirmities in order to invent extravagant remedies. What is surprising logically is that they always find dupes, even among the so-called "intellectuals"; the explanation for this is that these novelties come to fill a void that never should have been produced. In all these "methods," the point of departure is a false image of man; the goal of the training being the development — patterned after the "clairvoyance" of certain occultists — of "latent powers" or of an "expanded" or "liberated" personality. And since such an ideal does not exist — more especially as the premise is imaginary — the result of the adventure can only be a perversion; this is the price of a supersaturated rationalism — blown up to its extreme limit — namely an agnosticism devoid of all imagination.

9

*

* *

Strictly speaking, there is but one sole philosophy, the *Sophia Perennis;* it is also — envisaged in its integrality — the only religion. *Sophia* has two possible origins, one timeless and the other temporal: the first is "vertical" and discontinuous, and the second, "horizontal" and continuous; in other words, the first is like the rain that at any moment can descend from the sky; the second is like a stream that flows from a spring. Both modes meet and combine: metaphysical Revelation actualizes the intellective faculty, and once awakened, this gives rise to spontaneous and independent intellection.

The dialectic of the *Sophia Perennis* is "descriptive," not "syllogistic," which is to say that the affirmations are not the product of a real or imaginary "proof," even though they may make use of proofs — real in this case — by way of "illustration" and out of a concern for clarity and intelligibility. But the language of *Sophia* is above all symbolism in all its forms: thus the openness to the message of symbols is a gift proper to primordial man and his heirs in every age; *Spiritus autem ubi vult spirat.*

One of the paradoxes of our times is that esoterism, discreet by the force of things, finds itself obliged to assert itself publicly for the simple reason that there is no other remedy for the confusions of our time. For, as the Kabbalists say, "it is better to divulge Wisdom than to forget it."

Reflections on Ideological Sentimentalism

A doctrine can be described as sentimental not because it uses a symbolism of the feelings or because its language is more or less emotional, but because its point of departure is determined by a sentimental motive; indeed, it can happen that a doctrine founded on a particular aspect of reality does not try to avoid appeals to sentiment, whereas on the contrary, an illusory theory inspired by passion in its very axiom affects a rational or "icy" tone and displays an impeccable logic starting from its basic error; the "headless" character of this logic, however, will not escape the notice of those who know that logic has no validity except in virtue of the soundness — physical or metaphysical — of its foundation.

If we take the example of a doctrine in appearance completely intellectual and inaccessible to the emotions, namely Kantianism, considered as the archetype of theories seemingly divorced from all poetry, we shall have no difficulty in discovering that its starting point or "dogma" is reducible to a gratuitous reaction against all that lies beyond the reach of reason; it voices, therefore, a priori an instinctive revolt against truths which are rationally ungraspable and which are considered annoying on account of this very inaccessibility. All the rest is nothing but dialectical scaffolding, ingenious or "brilliant" if one wishes, but contrary to truth. What is crucial in Kantianism is not its *pro domo* logic and its few very limited lucidities, but the altogether "irrational" desire to limit intelligence; this results in a dehumanization of the intelligence and opens the door to all the inhuman aberrations of our century. In short, if to be man means the possibility of transcending oneself intellectually, Kantianism is the negation of all that is essentially and integrally human. Negations on this scale are always accompanied by a sort of moral fault which makes them less excusable than if it were merely a question of intellectual narrowness: the Kantists, failing to understand "dogmatic metaphysics," do not notice the enormous disproportion between the intellectual and human greatness of those they label as "metaphysical dogmatists" and the illusions which they attribute to them. Yet even if allowance be made for such a lack of understanding, it seems that any honest man ought to be sensitive, if only indirectly, to the human level of these "dogmatists" — what is evidence in metaphysics becomes "dogma" for those who do not understand it — and here is an extrinsic argument the extent of which cannot be neglected.

Whereas the metaphysician intends to come back to the "first word" — the word of primordial Intellection — the modern philosopher on the contrary wishes to have the "last word"; thus Comte imagines that after two inferior stages — namely "theology" and "metaphysics" — finally comes the "positive" or "scientific" stage which gloriously reduces itself to the most outward and coarse experiences; it is the stage of the rise of industry which, in the eyes of the philosopher, marks the summit of progress and of civilization. Like the "criticism" of Kant, the "positivism" of Comte starts from a sentimental instinct which wants to destroy everything in order to renew everything in the sense of a desacralized and totally "humanist" and profane world.

*
* *

12

Indignation against abuses brings with it the rejection of the positive principles which these abuses falsify; when sentimental reaction is given a philosophical codification, it perverts and impoverishes imagination. Error creates the stage-setting it requires in order to feel comfortable. The world becomes increasingly a system of stage-settings destined to limit and distort the imaginative faculty, imposing upon it an unshakable conviction that all this is "reality" and that there is no other; that all which is outside this system is but naive and culpable "romanticism." In the nineteenth century, and to a certain extent even since the Renaissance, people have in actual fact tried to create a universe in which there would be only man; in our time man has lost the initiative and is now slipping into a universe — or pseudo-universe — wherein only the machine is "real"; under these conditions one can no longer speak even of "humanism." In any case, man by attributing to himself his own self-sufficient reason, cannot remain what he is; if he no longer believes in that which transcends him and if he does not place his ideals above himself, he condemns himself to the subhuman.

It is difficult to deny, if one is still sensitive to true norms, that the machine tends to make man into its own counterpart; that it renders him violent, brutal, vulgar, quantitative and stupid like itself, and that all modern "culture" is affected thereby. This is what partly explains the cult of "sincerity" and the mystique of "commitment": one must be "sincere" because the machine is devoid of mystery and is as incapable of prudence as of generosity; one must be "committed" because the machine possesses no value apart from its productive capacity, or because it demands ceaseless surveillance and even complete "self-surrender"[1] and thus devours mankind and what is human; one must refrain

---

1. If it be objected that the same was true of the crafts of old, we would reply that there is a notable difference, in that these occupations displayed a properly human and thus contemplative character, and on that

from making oneself understood in literature and art because the machine does not so behave and because in the minds of its slaves and creatures its ugliness, clamor and implacability are mistaken for "reality." Above all, one must not have a God, since the machine has none or even usurps this role itself.[2]

*

* *

In the same connection, it is impossible not to pause over the practically crucial question of democratic and anti-theocratic ideology. A social theory, founded — as a reaction against particular abuses — on a desire for liberty, and imparting a disproportionate character to this claim in disregard of the real possibilities and interests of the individual, may develop without any dialectical inconsistency and thus give the impression of a perfect objectivity. The success of an ideology of this kind is explained by the fact that men who are unaware of the profound reasons of our terrestrial situations and for whom principles are merely "abstractions," allow themselves to be convinced by the violent voicing of a partially legitimate cause, without asking themselves if the ideology that is added to it is true or false; because we are hungry, the inaccessible date palm is a thief, and always has been. The passionate impulse — even when reasoning "coldly" — takes no account of the fact that a partial truth becomes false when one takes it out

account entailed neither the agitation nor the oppression characteristic of the machine age.

2. We would stress that in speaking of "God" we have in mind, not a concept which would be contrary — or inasmuch as it would be contrary — to Buddhism, but the "nirvanic" Reality which underlies all traditional concepts of the Absolute. It is this Reality which in the Mahayana expresses itself by the universal *Dharmakaya,* or in other words, by the *Ādi-Buddha.* In Japanese terms, the same function attaches to *Amitabha (Amida)* or *Vairochana (Dainichi),* according to the respective schools.

of its total context and imparts to it, by isolating it artificially, a quasi-unconditional significance.

In reality, the outward liberty of creatures is relative or conditional and cannot be otherwise; what tradition seeks to realize — and does realize to the extent permitted in our world of approximations — is a kind of balance between individual terrestrial freedom and the chances of celestial salvation; if one believes in eternal life, then a liberty which is disproportionate in relation to particular individual potentialities, and consequently compromises particular chances of salvation, is clearly not more desirable than a privation of liberty which does not compromise them. It is from this angle that one should consider whatever in traditional civilizations (if it is not a question of abuses) offends in too absolute a manner the sensibility of individualists who believe in nothing, or whose belief has no bearing on their intelligence and imagination; we say "too absolute" since it is normal for "legitimate" or "inevitable" ills to offend the sensibility of just men; but it is abnormal and in any case illegitimate that men draw erroneous conclusions from their own sensitivity.

The experience of the deceptive "liberty" which is propounded as an end in itself or as "art for art's sake" — as if one could be really free outside the truth and without inward liberty! — this experience, we say, is only in its beginning phase, although the world has already reaped some of its bitter fruits; for everything still human, normal and stable in the world survives only through the vitality of ancestral traditions — of "prejudices" if one so prefers — whether it be a matter of the West, molded by Christianity, or of any Nilotic or Amazonian tribe. To have some idea of what the free man of "tomorrow" might be like, the man starting from zero and "creating himself"[3] — but in reality the man of the machine which has escaped from his control

---

3. And creating the truth at the same time, of course.

— it suffices to take a glance at the very "existentialist" psychology of most youth. If the profound and "subconscious" imprints of tradition are removed from man, there remain finally only the stigmata of his fall and the unleashing of the infra-human.

Logically, democracy opposes tyranny, but in fact it leads to it. That is to say: since its reaction is sentimental — otherwise it would be centripetal and would tend towards theocracy, the only guarantee of a realistic liberty — it is merely an extreme which, by its unrealistic negation of authority and competence, inevitably calls forth another extreme and a new authoritarian reaction, one which this time is authoritarian and tyrannical in its very principle. The democratic illusion appears above all in the following traits: in democracy, truth amounts to the belief of the majority; it is the latter which practically speaking "creates" the truth; democracy itself is true only insofar as, and as long as, the majority believes in it, and thus it carries in its breast the germs of its suicide. Authority, which one is obliged to tolerate on pain of anarchy, lives at the mercy of the electors, hence the impossibility of real government. The ideal of "liberty" makes a prisoner of the government, a prisoner constantly obliged to follow the interests of various pressure groups; the electoral campaigns themselves prove that the aspirants to authority must dupe the electors, and the means of this dupery are so vulgar and stupid and constitute such a degradation of the people that this alone should suffice to reduce the myth of modern democracy to naught. This does not necessarily mean that no form of democracy is possible; but then it is primarily a question of communities of limited size — especially nomadic ones — and also of an inwardly aristocratic and theocratic democracy, and not of a secular egalitarianism imposed upon large sedentary populations.

We may also stress the following: it can happen that a man is intelligent and competent, or that a minority is; but it cannot happen that the majority is intelligent and competent, or "more intelligent" or "more competent." The adage *vox populi vox Dei* has no meaning except in a religious framework which confers a function of "medium" on the crowds; they then express themselves not by thought but by intuition and under the influence of Heaven, unless it is a matter of the competence pertaining to every sane-minded, God-fearing man, so that the feeling of the majority coincides in any case with what may be called "the good." It is clear that a people as a collective vehicle of religion possesses a positive character — all religions testify to this — and is thus instinctively right in the face of pernicious and impious exceptions.[4] A people is what it is, both in good and evil; it has not the virtues of the "center," but it may have those of the "totality," on condition that the "center" determine it. Besides, the word "people" itself admits of two meanings: it denotes either the majority, as distinguished from the intellectual and aristocratic elite, or the total or integral collectivity, comprising the majority and the elite at one and the same time; in this last sense, it is self-evident that the government — apart from its celestial origin — derives from the "people" itself and that the chivalric and sacerdotal elite are an expression of the popular genius.

Let us include here a word on "free thought," or more exactly on the quasi-moral obligation currently placed upon all men to "think for themselves"; this demand is incompatible with human nature, for the normal and virtuous man, as a member of a social and traditional collectivity, generally takes into account the limits of his competence. One of two things is possible: either the man is exceptionally gifted on a given plane and therefore nothing can prevent him from thinking in an original way, which he will moreover do consonantly with tradition precisely because

---

4. It can also be mistaken when it is a question of phenomena exceeding the bounds of exoterism, even though there is an aspect of esoterism that is anchored in the people, notably in the handicrafts.

his intelligence enables him to grasp the necessity of this consonance; or the man is of average or mediocre intelligence, either on some particular plane or in a general way, and then he will rely on the judgements of those more competent than himself, which in his case is the most intelligent thing he can do. The mania for detaching the individual from the intellectual hierarchy, or in other words, for individualizing him intellectually, is a violation of his nature and is practically equivalent to the abolition of intelligence and also of the virtues, without which real understanding cannot be fully actualized. It only leads to anarchy and to the codification of the inability to think.

*

* *

A very "contemporary" variant of the ideological sentimentalism which we have in mind, one that is prevalent even among "believers," is the demagogic obsession with purely "social" values. Formerly, when everybody was religious, poverty preserved the poor from hypocrisy, or from a certain kind of hypocrisy. In our time, poverty too often leads to unbelief and envy — especially in countries which have been industrialized or otherwise contaminated by the industrialist mentality — with the result that rich and poor are on equal terms; the hypocrisy of one side is answered by the impiety of the other. It is profoundly unjust to prefer this new shortcoming of the poor to the habitual, and traditionally stigmatized, shortcoming of the rich and to excuse the impiety of the former because of their poverty without excusing the latter because of their riches: if the poor are victims of their estate, the rich are equally so of theirs; if poverty confers the right to impiety, riches equally confer the right to a simulation of piety. If the one side is to be pitied spiritually, the other is to be pitied and excused on the same grounds, seeing that the difference between them rests solely on completely exterior and easily reversible situations, and not on anything fundamental in the nature

18

of man. One can only prefer the poor when they are better than the rich through their spiritual sincerity, their patience and their secret heroism — such poor always exist, as also rich men who are detached from their riches — and not when they are worse by their unbelief, envy and hatred. The Christians persecuted by Nero suffered far more grievously than any underpaid workmen of today, without theology thereby granting them the right to cease believing in God or to scorn His laws; tradition has never admitted this kind of economic blackmail addressed to God.

In short, three questions determine the human problem, in spite of humanitarian and progressivist sentimentalities: if all men were exempt from material cares, would the world be saved? Assuredly not; for evil resides above all in man himself, as experience proves.[5] If all men set themselves to supplying the needs of others with regard to their physical well-being conceived apart from religion, would the world be saved? No, certainly not, since the very basis of the problem would remain untouched. If all men thought of God, to the point of forgetting their own well-being, would the world be saved? Yes, certainly; "and all these things shall be added unto you," says the Gospel, which is to say that the reform of man would ipso facto bring about a reform of the world, and even a beneficial reaction on the part of the whole cosmic environment.

Progressivism is the wish to eliminate effects without wishing to eliminate their causes; it is the wish to abolish calamities without realizing that they are nothing other than what man himself is; they necessarily result from his metaphysical ignorance, or his lack of love of God. Account must also be taken of this: God cannot primarily "take an interest" in the well-being of creatures, since He wants their

---

5. In economically supersaturated countries, imbued with social idealism and "humanitarian" psychoanalysis, the moral problem is in no way solved; privileged youth shows itself capable of crime without having the excuse of poverty.

souls and their imperishable good and not the transitory things of the material world. If God also wants our earthly well-being it is not because He regards it as an end in itself, but because a certain happiness is the normal condition of man who, however, is essentially created with a view to eternal values. God takes interest in our well-being to the extent that we may profit from it in view of Him, and not otherwise; but outside this "interest" — if this word be permissible here in a provisional way — God "sendeth rain on the just and on the unjust." Together with bread, truth must be imparted, since "man shall not live by bread alone"; hunger together with truth is better than an easy life together with error. Well-being is there to serve our ultimate ends as clay is there to make vessels.

Some people readily accuse of "selfishness" the contemplative preoccupied with his salvation, and maintain that instead of saving oneself one should save others; but this is firstly hypocritical and secondly absurd because, on the one hand, it is not from excess of virtue that those who argue thus refuse sanctification, and on the other hand, it is impossible to save others, since one can only know and will with one's own knowledge and one's own will; if it is possible to contribute to saving others, it is only by virtue of one's own salvation. No man has ever been of service to anyone by remaining attached to his own faults out of "altruism"; whoever neglects his own salvation certainly will save no one else. To mask passions and spiritual indifference behind good works is a proof of hypocrisy.

The social interest can only be defined in terms of the truth; it is impossible to define truth in terms of the social.

*
* *

Too often one hears the reproach of "sentimentality" leveled at those who protest, not against some necessary evil, but against baseness; this reproach, even if it accidentally coincides with the truth from a purely psychological

20

point of view, is however completely unjustified when it is designed to reduce intelligent reactions to their possible emotional concomitants. For: that the strong attack the weak is sometimes an unavoidable evil and even in certain respects an effect of a natural law,[6] provided that the means used not violate the norms of nature as in mechanized wars, and provided that force not serve intrinsically false ideas, which would be yet another anomaly. But that the strong should crush the weak by means of an interested hypocrisy with its accompanying baseness is neither natural nor inevitable; it is gratuitous and even infamous to label as "sentimentalism" all opinion which condemns these methods; political "realism" may justify violence, but never villainies. But there is not only this alternative; there are still facts which, without being in themselves either necessary evils or turpitudes properly speaking, are rather due to a distressing and senseless thoughtlessness, abuses brought about by prejudice, complacency, lack of imagination and unconscious habit; such things are inevitable, not in the particular but on the whole, the collective man of the "dark age" being what he is. In this case, to be distressed by a particular happening does not necessarily imply a reprehensible sentimentality; what would be so is to be indignant against the very existence of such phenomena within an ancient civilization and to wish to destroy the latter for the sake of abolishing the happenings in question.

When we set out to compare Antiquity with our own times two extremes are noticeable: on the one hand we have the abstract and marmoreal hardness of the ancients, founded on the law of natural selection and on the aristo-

---

6. We are referring above all to tribal or feudal wars, or wars of expansion of the traditional civilizations. Some will object that there have always been machines and that a bow is nothing else, which is as false as to claim that a circle is a sphere or a drawing is a statue. Here there is a difference of dimensions whose causes are profound and not merely quantitive.

cratic virtues of gods and heroes, and on the other hand we have the democratic excesses of our day, such as the reign of inferiors, the cult of mediocrity and vulgarity, the sentimentalist protection, not of the weak, but of weakness and defects,[7] the psychological softness towards all forms of laxity and vice, immorality upheld in the name of liberty and sincerity, stupidity and idle chatter masquerading as "culture," the scorn of wisdom and the neutralization of religion, and then the misdeeds of an atheistical science that leads to overpopulation, degeneration and catastrophe. Now these aberrations allow us, if not to condone the faults of the ancients, at least to understand their fundamental outlook; it will then be realized that there are no grounds for unconditionally condemning this outlook in itself in the name of a so-called "moral progress" such as in reality only leads to the opposite excesses, to say the least.[8] Like all social dreaming, that of egalitarianism presupposes a fragmentary world made up exclusively of honest people who think only of kneading their bread in peace without being molested either by wolves or by the gods; now the wolves are to be found within the "good people" themselves, and as for the gods, abettors of "fanaticism," it suffices to put them aside for devils to come in and take their place.

Nothing could be more false than to claim that the Middle Ages were as good as our era is bad; the Middle Ages were bad because the abuses which distorted the traditional principles were carried to their uttermost in relation to the possibilities of the time; without these abuses the modern reaction — the Renaissance and the Reformation — could not have happened. But compared with our times the

7. The protection of the weak has always been practiced, in one form or another, in civilizations which still remain healthy.

8. Collectivist dictatorships have sprung from democracy and re-edit its prejudices in their own fashion in the sense that they intend to realize the so-called humanitarian ideals by Babylonian means.

Middle Ages were nevertheless "better," and even "good," given the fact that they were still ruled by principles.

At every turn we are told that we must "be contemporary" in our ideas, and that the fact of "looking back" or "hanging back" amounts to treason in respect to the "categorical imperative" which is our own century; but no one has ever been able to give the least justification or plausibility to this grotesque demand. "There is no right superior to that of the truth," say the Hindus; and if two and two make four, this certainly is not so in terms of some particular time or other. Everything which goes on in our time forms part of this time, including opposition to its tendencies; the copying of Antiquity formed part of the Renaissance outlook, and if in our time some people look towards the Middle Ages or the East, one is bound to register the fact as also belonging to the period in which we live. It is the nature of things which definitively determines what our time is and is not; it is certainly not for men to decide what has the right to be true and what does not.

*
* *

Philosophical "vitalism" also dissimulates — under the guise of an impeccable logic — a fallacious and properly infra-human line of thought. The devotees of "life," for whom religion, or wisdom, is only an unintelligible, artificial and morbid kill-joy, overlook above all the following truths: namely that human intelligence is capable of objectifying life and of opposing itself to it to a certain extent, which fact cannot be devoid of meaning, everything having its sufficient cause; that it is by this capacity of objectification and opposition versus the subjective that man is man, life and pleasure being common also to all infra-human creatures; that there is not only life but also death, not only pleasure but also pain, of which man alone can give account a priori; that man ought to follow his nature as animals follow theirs, and that in following it fully he tends to transcend appearances and to give them a significance which surpasses their shifting plane and unites them in a same stable and universal reality. For man is intelligence, and intelligence is the transcending of forms and the realization of the invisible Essence; to say human intelligence is to say absoluteness and transcendence.

Of all earthly creatures, man alone knows: firstly, that pleasure is contingent and ephemeral; and secondly, that it is not shared by all, which is to say that other egos do not enjoy the pleasures of our ego and that, whatever our enjoyment, there are always other creatures who suffer, and vice versa; and this proves that pleasure is not everything, nor is life. Religion and metaphysics spring much more deeply from our specifically human nature — a supernatural nature, precisely, in its depths — than the characteristics man shares with animals and plants.

To refute an error does not mean ignorance of the necessity for its existence; the two things are situated on different planes. We do not accept error, but we accept its existence since "offenses must needs come."

*

* *

We said that a doctrine merits the epithet "sentimental," not because it makes use of a symbolism of the feelings or because it reflects incidentally in its form the sentiments of the writer who expounds it, but because its point of departure is determined more by feeling than by objective reality, which means that the latter is violated by the former. To this definition we must add a reservation in favor of the traditional doctrines, or some of them: strictly speaking, a true doctrine could be qualified by use of the word "sentimental" when sentiment is introduced into the very substance of that doctrine, while limiting the truth, by force of circumstance, on account of the "subjective" and affective character of sentimentality as such; it is in this sense that Guénon spoke of the presence of a sentimental element in the Semitic exoterisms, while pointing out that it is this element which causes the incompatibilities between dogmas of different origins. But in this case, the term "sentimental" cannot mean that the doctrine itself originates in a sentimental and therefore human reaction, as happens with profane ideologies; on the contrary, here the marriage between truth and sentiment is a providential and beneficial concession to certain psychological predispositions, so that the epithet in question is only applicable on condition that one specifies that it concerns orthodox doctrines.

The Intellect — that kind of static Revelation, permanent in principle and "supernaturally natural" — is not opposed to any possible expression of the Real; it is situated beyond sentiment, imagination, memory and reason, but it can at the same time enlighten and determine all of these since they are like its individualized ramifications, ordained as receptacles to receive the light from on high and to translate it according to their respective capacities. The positive quintessence of sentiment is love; and love, to the extent that it transcends itself in the direction of its supernatural source, is the love of man for God and of God for man, and finally it is Beatitude without origin and without end.

Usurpations of Religious Feeling

One of the abuses indirectly bequeathed to us by the Renaissance is the confusion, in one and the same sentimental cult or in one and the same "humanism," of religion and fatherland: this amalgam is all the more deplorable in that it occurs in men who are supposed to represent traditional values and who thus compromise what they should defend. Doubtless a believer does not always have the direct duty to preach about the truth that gives meaning to life, but he certainly never has the right to adulterate it for entirely human reasons which cease to be valid a few miles away; by seeking to justify given passions in the name of religion, one merely succeeds in rendering the latter unintelligible and sometimes even odious, a result which proves that its cause is anything but harmless, and far from deserving in the way of blame merely an unconcerned and compliant indulgence.

It is quite obvious that in order to be able to determine the rights of earthly things — and we regret that this is not a truism — it is necessary to start from the axiomatic truth that the value of man and of things lies in their adequation to the integral Real and in their capacity to participate directly or indirectly in this end; the role of the contemplative man is constantly to look towards this Real and ipso facto to communicate to society the perfume of this vision; a perfume both of life and death, and indispensable for any relative well-being to which the world here below may be entitled. It is necessary, therefore, to start from the idea that spirituality alone — and with it the religion which necessarily is its framework — constitutes an absolute good; it is the spiritual, not the temporal, which culturally, socially and politically is the criterion of all other values.

As regards the de facto and de jure limits of the patriotic sentiment, it is proper to recall first of all that there is fatherland and then fatherland: there is that of earth and that of Heaven; the latter is the prototype and measure of the former, giving it its meaning and legitimacy. Thus in the Gospel teaching, the love of God has priority over, and consequently may contradict, the love of close relatives, without there being the least offense against charity; the creature, moreover, must be loved "in God," which means that love never belongs to the creature exclusively. Christ cared only for the heavenly Fatherland which "is not of this world"; this is sufficient, not to deny the natural fact of an earthly fatherland, but to abstain from any abusive — and above all illogical — worship of one's country of origin. If Christ repudiated temporal attachments, he nonetheless admitted the rights of nature, in the realm where they apply, rights which are eminently relative and which must never be erected into idols; this is a theme that Saint Augustine has dealt with in a most masterly way, at least from one point of view, in his *Civitas Dei*. Normal patriotism is both determined and limited by eternal values; "it is not puffed up" and does not pervert the spirit; unlike chauvinism, it is not an official disregard for humility and charity or an anaesthesia for a whole sector of the intelligence; remaining within its own limits, it is capable of giving rise to the most splendid virtues without becoming a parasite on religion.

One has to be on guard against abusive interpretations of the historic past; the work of Joan of Arc had nothing to do with modern nationalism, especially as the saint followed the impulsion, not of a natural patriotism — this would have been legitimate — but of a will of Heaven, which saw far ahead. For centuries, France had been the pivot of Catholicism; an English France in the long run would have meant a Protestant Europe and the end of the Catholic Church; this is what Joan's "voices" wished to prevent. The absence in Joan of all passion, her serene words with regard to the English, corroborate fully what has just been said and more than suffice to defend the saint from any retrospective imposture.[1]

If it be permitted to interpolate here a more general consideration related to the abusive annexation of historical examples, it may be said that a very common and particularly annoying error is to believe that in our own age one can do everything that was done in the Middle Ages and Antiquity; but before speaking of this, it is appropriate first to mention the opposite error, according to which "our time" gives us the right to despise as "out of date" what was timeless in the Middle Ages, and which consequently has not ceased to be so in essentials; this is a question of things or attitudes which concern, not the man of such and such a time, but man as such. Indeed, the attitude of modern men towards the past only too often comprises a double error: on the one hand, they consider that certain forms with a timeless content are irreconcilable with the mental conditions of what they call "our time"; on the other hand, in order to introduce some reform or simplification, they readily refer to what was done in Antiquity or the Middle Ages, as if cyclic conditions always remained the same and as if there were not, from the point of view of spiritual fluidity and inspiration, a progressive impoverishment or lowering of possibilities. Religion — for it is religion that is mostly in question — is like a growing tree which has a root, a trunk, branches and leaves and in which there is no element of chance — an oak never produces anything other

1. Likewise Joan's standard was a completely different thing from a revolutionary flag which unites in the same profane cult both believers and unbelievers.

29

than acorns — and whose order of growing cannot blindly be inverted; such a growth is not an "evolution" in the progressivistic sense of the word, although, in parallel with the descent towards exteriorization and hardening, there is obviously a deployment on the level of mental formulation and art. The so-called return to a primitive simplicity is really at the antipodes of this very simplicity precisely because we are no longer at the origin and also because modern man is affected by a singular lack of sense of proportion; our ancestors would never have conceived that it was enough to see in an error "our time" in order to concede to it rights not only over things, but even over intelligence.

But let us return to the notion of fatherland: in concrete terms, the fatherland is not necessarily a State, but the country or countryside in which one was born and the people or ethnic or cultural group to which one belongs.[2] It is only natural for man to love his place of origin, just as it is natural, in normal conditions, that a man should love his parents or that spouses should love one another and their children; and it is no less natural that every man should contribute, according to his functions and his means, to the defense of his country or of his people when they are attacked. Assuredly it cannot be maintained that it is always illegitimate for one nation to attack another, but in this case it is illegitimate — let it be observed in passing — to indiscriminately force all citizens to participate in such an attack, since traditionally, or let us say according to a natural right, a mass call-up is legitimate only in case of national distress.[3]

---

2. Thus the real fatherland of an Algerian Moslem may be not so much the Algerian State as the Islamic Maghreb, irrespective of what its accidental subdivisions may be; and this Maghreb is an ancient and vital part of the Moslem world.

3. Even people as warlike as the Indians of North America knew nothing of "general mobilization," each individual having the right not

But nationalistic patriotism, precisely, is not content with natural positions: according to it, the fatherland becomes in practice an integral part of religion, even if it oppresses the latter. This is not to say that the fatherland is not more than an earthly accident without a spiritual meaning, far from that: it is evident that the fatherland may assume a religious value to the extent that it is the concrete and traditional vehicle of religion; this is beyond doubt the case of the Vedic Lands, ancient Israel, the Middle Empire, Shintoist Japan, *Dār al-Islām* and other analogous instances; and this obviously applied likewise to the ancient "Christendom," then to the Holy Roman Empire and to a certain extent to the Kingdom of France, "elder daughter of the Church";[4] it is noteworthy that the king of France considered that he derived his authority from David by sacramental analogy, while the Emperor of Germany derived his from Caesar, by historical continuity.

The sacred character of a nation depends, not on the sanctity of its citizens, this is obvious, but on the traditional integrity of its regime; what makes it impossible to equate a secular State with a "Holy Land" is precisely the confession-

to participate in a warlike expedition; this was often the case with medicine men and recognized hunters. The same held true in the case of the Israelites: "And it shall be, when ye are come nigh unto the battle, that the priest shall approach and speak unto the people, . . . and the officers shall speak unto the people, saying, What man is there that hath built a new house and hath not dedicated it? let him go and return to his house, lest he die in the battle, and another man dedicate it. And what man is he that hath planted a vineyard, . . . let him also go and return unto his house. . . . And what man is there that hath betrothed a wife, . . . let him go and return unto his house. . . . What man is there that is fearful and fainthearted? let him go and return unto his house, lest his brethren's heart faint as well as his heart" (Deut. 20:2-8).

4. Let us also mention "Holy Russia," which could be considered as heir to Byzantium, the "New Rome and New Jerusalem," and as the predestined protector of the whole Eastern Church. Analogous remarks apply to Abyssinia, since it is the only sovereign Empire of monophysite confession.

ally "neutral" and therefore heterogeneous and profane character of modern civilization. There are two idolatries which are incompatible with the sacred character of a nation: one is civilizationism, the other is nationalism; the former, which is "pagan" and worldly in essence, dates from the irruption of Prometheanism that was the Renaissance, and the latter, which is secular, racist and democratic in essence, dates from the French Revolution, which itself was a kind of Renaissance but in vulgar, not aristocratic mode. Now it is precisely these two frameworks, "civilization" and "fatherland," that many people lay claim to in the name of tradition, without realizing that this involves more than one contradiction: firstly, and this is essential, religion is something sacred and thus cannot fit in with entirely profane ideologies and institutions; secondly, "civilization" would have itself essentially objective, since it is rationalistic and scientistic, whereas the nationalist and racist "fatherland" on the contrary is subjective by definition, whence an absurd and hypocritical mixture of scientism and romanticism.

Profane patriotism improperly mixed with religion is a luxury which is all the more useless in that it substitutes itself for a normal patriotism, and all the more pernicious in that it fatally compromises the prestige of religion. Here it is a case of two religions being confused in fact, one of them true and the other false, and this doubtless explains to some extent the reluctance shown by Heaven in coming to the aid of a tradition which has already been betrayed in various ways by its own adherents. According to nationalistic and "Jacobin" patriotism, the fatherland never commits a crime, or nothing is a crime if it is done in the name of the fatherland; or again, if it does act badly, it is a crime to reproach it for this.[5] The fatherland-nation is erected into

5. But it is never wrong to proclaim aloud, or to carve in marble, the tale of other peoples' misdeeds, taking them out of their context of

a transcendent value, and the patriotic sentiment of others is possibly trampled under foot, even while an unsullied "loyalty" is still expected of them; one despises foreign peoples, but one still wishes to be liked by them. What we reproach chauvinistic patriots for is certainly not their consciousness of the real values of their country, but their blindness toward those of certain other countries — it is a question of political and sentimental interest — and even toward the most elementary rights of other peoples, whereas the said patriots erect these same rights into a universal law and make of them a principle of life. This brings to mind those so-called "peace treaties," conceived in the name of "self-determination," which replace ancient oppressions by new ones while at the same time maintaining such of the past subjugations as do not inconvenience any of the signatories.

*

* *

The extreme detachment of Christ with regard to his fatherland, which he neither saved from Roman domination nor even from destruction by the Romans, ought to be a cause for reflection among the partisans of unconditional patriotism; of course we do not maintain that every country is necessarily in the same position as ancient Judea, but like Judea, no fatherland has an overriding value unless it is the vehicle of an unbetrayed spiritual patrimony. There is doubtless no tradition that has not been betrayed in part, but in this respect there are eminent differences of degree — a circle not being a sphere and a square not being a cube, despite the analogy — and after a certain degree of denial, a fatherland ceases to be sacred in any case.

circumstances and without taking into account the laws of collective psychology lying behind them, in any given case.

*

* *

Religion, when it is not neutralized by an adulteration which diminishes it and by concessions which debase it, and provided that, on the contrary, it be founded on what constitutes its true nature and reason for existence, namely our eternal destiny whose evidence we carry in the very substance of our spirit — religion then, comprises in its heart the answer to every possible human question and the solution to every real problem. A problem is real if it touches our integral nature and our final interests; an impasse due to our refusal to accept the truth and with it the fatalities of earthly existence is not a true problem. All our miseries are the effect of our separation from the Divine Principle, or from the "Self" as the Vedantists would say. Now religion is concerned with this cause rather than with its effects, or to be more accurate, it is concerned with the effects in function of their cause; it strives to abolish this separation — the saints succeed in this and show the way — but its aim could not possibly be to cure the effects individually and with a "worldly" intention, nor does it try to make the world cease being the world. One cannot eliminate the consequences of sin without eliminating sin itself; if one could do so for a moment, nothing would be solved and everything would have to be started all over again, since sin itself would remain;[6] the great betrayal of the progressivists is to deliberately ignore this and to shut their eyes to what constitutes the quintessence of the human condition. Religion is reproached for being unable to solve the "problems of our time," but it is not understood, firstly that religion

6. By "sin" must be understood our separation from the Divine Center insofar as this shows itself in attitudes or acts; the essence of sin is a forgetting of the Absolute, which is at the same time the Infinite and the Perfect, and this forgetting coincides with centrifugal passion and at the same time with egoistic hardening.

has in view only the problems of all times, and secondly that no one will be able to solve new problems, if only because each solution, on this plane or level, gives rise to newer problems;[7] finally, people fail to see that religion alone would be qualified, in principle, not to do impossible things, but to do what could and ought to be done, whether this be in conformity with current prejudices or not. The key to the world and its destiny lies within ourselves, and this is the point of view of religion and of every undertaking proportioned to our total nature; whoever can do the greater can in principle do the lesser, and the latter has no meaning except in function of the former. "The kingdom of heaven is within you,"[8] says the Gospel; no one can say it better.

7. In the nineteenth century, the machine — the kind which combined "iron" and "fire" — was supposed to solve once and for all the problem of work; serums were to abolish illness, and so on. Now the actual results prompt the remark that a rainmaker must neither be ineffective, nor provoke a flood. It is moreover contradictory to want to abolish work and then to glorify it to the point of making a religion of it.
8. This means, not that Heaven is something subjective — *quod absit* — but that access to Heaven passes through the human subject.

The Impossible Convergence

According to the unanimous conviction of early Christendom and of all the other traditional branches of humanity, the cause of suffering in the world is the internal disharmony of man — sin, if so preferred — and not just a lack of science and organization. Neither progress nor any tyranny will ever bring about an end of suffering; only the sanctification of all men could succeed in this, were it in fact possible to realize such a state of things and thus to transform the world into a community of contemplatives and into a new earthly paradise. This certainly does not mean that man should not, in conformity with his nature and with simple good sense, attempt to overcome the evils he encounters in the course of his life; for this he requires no injunction whether divine or human. But to seek to establish a certain well-being in a country with God in view is one thing, and to seek to realize perfect happiness on earth apart from God is another; the latter aim is in any case foredoomed to failure, precisely because the lasting elimination of our miseries is dependent upon our conformity to the Divine Equilibrium, or upon our establishment in the "kingdom of Heaven which is within you." As long as men have not realized sanctifying inwardness, the abolition of earthly trials is not only impossible, it is not even desirable; because the sinner — "exteriorized" man — has need of suffering in order to expiate his faults and tear himself away from sin, or in order to escape the "outwardness" from

37

which sin derives.[1] From the spiritual point of view, which alone takes account of the true cause of our calamities, evil is not by definition what causes us to suffer, it is that which — even when accompanied by a maximum of comfort or of ease, or of "justice" so-called — thwarts a maximum of souls as regards their final end.

The whole problem is reducible finally to the following nucleus of questions: what is the good of eliminating only the effects, and not the cause, of evil? What is the good of eliminating these effects if the cause remains and continues to produce similar effects indefinitely? What is the good of eliminating the effects of evil to the detriment of the elimination of the cause itself? What is the good of eliminating the effects but at the same time exchanging the cause for another far more pernicious one, namely hatred of the supernatural and a passion for the worldly?

In a word: if one combats the calamities of this world without regard for the total truth and the ultimate good, one will be creating incomparably greater calamities, starting, in fact, with the denial of this truth and the forfeiture of this good. Those who intend to liberate man from an age-old "frustration" are in fact the ones who impose on him the most radical and irreparable of all frustrations.

The *Civitas Dei* and worldly progressivism therefore cannot converge, contrary to what is imagined by those who strive to accommodate the religious message to profane illusions and agitations. "Whoso gathereth not with me, scattereth": this saying, like many others, seems to have

1. From this idea follows the obligation for men, in the majority of archaic tribes, to be warriors, and thus to be continually risking their lives on the battlefield; the same point of view is to be found in the warrior castes of all the great peoples. Without the heroic virtues, so it is believed, man becomes decadent and the whole of society degenerates. The only man for whom escape from this vicissitude is possible is the saint, which amounts to saying that if all men were contemplatives the hard law of heroism would not be necessary. Only the hero and the saint reach Valhalla, Elysium, or the heaven of the Kamis.

become a dead letter, doubtless because it does not belong to "our time." Nevertheless, as a recent encyclical* tells us: "The Church must examine the signs of the times and interpret them in the light of the Gospel"; yet meanwhile it is the exact opposite that is being done.

*

* *

"Seek ye first the Kingdom of God and his righteousness, and all else shall be added unto you": this sentence is the very key to the problem of our earthly condition, as is also that other one telling us that "the Kingdom of Heaven is within you." Or further, to recall another teaching from the Gospel: evil will only be overcome by "fasting and prayer," that is to say, by detachment from the world, which is "outward" and by attachment to Heaven, which is "inward."

To the question: "What is sin?" it may be replied that this term refers to two levels or dimensions: the first of these requires that one should "obey the commandments," and the second, in accordance with the words of Christ to the rich young man, that one should "follow Me," which is to say, that one should establish oneself in the "inward dimension" and so realize contemplative perfection; the example of Mary takes precedence over that of Martha. Now, suffering in the world is due not only to sin in the elementary sense of the word, but above all to the sin of "outwardness," which moreover fatally gives rise to all the others. A perfect world would be, not merely one where men abstained from sins of action and omission, as did the rich young man, but a world composed of men who live "towards the Inward" and are firmly established in the knowledge — and consequently in the love — of that Invis-

---

*This article having been written during the reign of Pope John XXIII, the encyclical referred to belongs to that era. (Translator's note)

ible which transcends and includes all things. Three degrees must here be observed: the first is abstention from sin-as-act, such as murder, theft, lying and the non-performance of sacred duties; the second is abstention from sin-as-vice, such as pride, passion, avarice; the third is abstention from sin-as-a-state, which is to say, from the "outwardness" that is both a dispersion and a hardening and that gives rise to all vices and all transgressions. The absence of this sin-as-a-state is nothing other than "love of God" or "inwardness," whatever the spiritual mode thereof. Only this inwardness would be capable of regenerating the world, and that is why it has been said that the world would have come to an end long ago but for the presence of the saints, whether visible or hidden.

It is sin-as-vice and, with all the more reason, sin-as-a-state that constitute intrinsic sin; these two degrees meet in pride, a symbolic notion which includes everything that imprisons the soul in outwardness and keeps it away from the Divine Life. As regards the first degree — that of transgression — there is here no intrinsic sin except in relation to the intention and therefore to a real opposition to a revealed Law. It may happen that a forbidden act becomes permissible in certain circumstances, for one is always allowed to lie to a brigand or to kill in legitimate defense; but apart from such circumstances, an illegal act is always connected with intrinsic sin; it is assimilable to sin-as-vice and by that very fact to sin-as-a-state, the latter being none other than "hardness of heart" or the state of "paganism," to use Biblical language.

The impossible convergence is, in point of fact, the alliance between the principle of good and organized sin; it is the idea that the powers of this world, which are necessarily sinful powers, should organize sin with the aim of abolishing the effects of sin. It appears that the new pastoral message is attempting precisely to speak the language of the "world," which has now come to be treated as an honorable entity without there being the slightest discernible reason for this unexpected promotion. Now to wish to speak the language of the "world," or the language of "our time" — another definition which studiously avoids being one — amounts to making truth speak the language of error or virtue the language of vice. The whole problem of pastoral communication in search of "a language" reduces itself in practice to the following feat: how to speak Latin so that people may think it is Chinese, or in other words, so that they do not notice that it is Latin? Nothing is more dubious than the expression "to speak the language of someone or other" or else "to speak the language of one's time." With the relativistic adulteration that this really implies, one may perhaps win adherents, but no one will be "converted"; no one will be enlightened and no one will be called to saving inwardness.[2]

To understand religion is to accept it without imposing impertinent conditions; imposing conditions on it is evidently to misunderstand it and to render it subjectively ineffective: an absence of haggling is part of the integrity of faith. To impose conditions — whether at the level of individual or social "well-being" or at the level of the liturgy which one wishes to be as flat and trivial as possible — is to be in fundamental ignorance of what religion is, of what God is and what man is. It amounts to reducing religion from the outset to a neutral and inoperative background such as it could never be and to taking away from it in advance all its rights and its whole reason for existing. Profane humanitarianism, with which official religion is

---

2. "But into whatsoever city ye enter, and they receive you not, go your ways out into the streets of the same and say, even the very dust of your city, which cleaveth on us, we do wipe off against you. Notwithstanding, be ye sure of this, that the Kingdom of God is come nigh unto you. But I say unto you, that it shall be more tolerable in that day for Sodom than for that city" (Luke 10:10-12). This passage, like the one that forbids the "casting of pearls before swine," clearly shows that everything has its limits.

trying more and more to identify itself, is incompatible with the total truth, and consequently also with true charity, for the simple reason that the material well-being of earthly man is not the whole of well-being and does not in fact coincide with a comprehensive interest of the immortal human person.

"Seek ye first the Kingdom of God . . ." To recall this truth over and over again is the first duty of all men of religion; if there is a truth which is particularly apt for "our time," it is this one more than any other.

To be above all reproach for inconsequence, hypocrisy and betrayal, it is not enough to belong to a religion, one must belong to it "in spirit and in truth."

"O Children of Israel, remember My Grace that I have conferred upon you and keep your covenant with Me; then will I keep My covenant with you" (Koran, II:40). This verse expresses a truth which is too often lost sight of, namely that such a pact is necessarily of a unilateral nature, for the simple reason that man cannot place himself on the same ground of reality as the Absolute which alone is real, and that in consequence any relationship between God and man, or between the Absolute and the relative, is unilateral a priori. If it is true that a covenant or an agreement of any kind is inconceivable without reciprocity, this reciprocity is nonetheless unrealizable between God and man, except at the cost of certain conditions that man must fulfill and that confer upon him, in regard to God, a stability symbolically conformable with the divine immutability; and this immutability is, in regard to man, the absolute "fidelity" of God. Man can benefit from this fidelity only thanks to his spiritual stability, which amounts to saying that in a covenant with God the position of man is conditional; indeed it is only on condition that he be in a certain state, or conscious of a certain reality, that man can enter into or remain in a relationship of alliance with God. For God, and He alone, is essentially and absolutely Himself, whereas man, a being who does not bear within himself his sufficient reason, is not "himself" by means of himself, but uniquely through his participation in the immutable Ipseity of God. The unconditional nature of the divine promise that consecrates a covenant clearly refers to the absolute fidelity of God and not to the potential infidelity of man. In other words, the promise is absolute insofar as it comes from God and not insofar as it becomes without an object when man is no longer the same "himself," and having thus lost the state of grace — that is to say, no longer fulfilling the conditions upon which, in God's eyes, he is "himself" — has become another being than the one to whom the divine promise is addressed.

Every covenant establishing the origin of a tradition, however unconditional its formulation may be, thus necessarily implies a reservation concerning man who, at the moment of the covenant and through its sanctifying power, has become symbolically absolute; it is only insofar as the relative is a mirror of the Absolute and hence actually represents, to a degree that may be said to be supernatural, a kind of symbolic aspect of the Absolute,[3] that there can be a common measure — represented by the covenant — between God and man.

---

3. Just as every human being represents such an aspect in a natural way, and this by reason of the analogical correspondences between the microcosm, the macrocosm and what might be called the "Metacosm."

Art, Its Duties and Its Rights

Because of his objective and hence total intelligence, *homo sapiens* is necessarily *homo faber;* he not only has the gift of speech, he also has the gift of mental and artistic creation. It is natural for man to imitate nature, for being "made in the image of God," he has the capacity and the right to create; but it is not natural for him to imitate nature in a total fashion, since he is man, not God. This is what is ignored by naturalistic art, which by wishing to imitate living beings in an absolute manner, reaches a dead point where the work becomes something useless and no longer fits into any spiritual context; it is a kind of sin in that it promises what it cannot fulfill, since it is incapable of animating bodies that require life.

Art has a function that is both magical and spiritual: magical, it renders present principles, powers and also things that it attracts by virtue of a "sympathetic magic"; spiritual, it exteriorizes truths and beauties in view of our interiorization, of our return to the "kingdom of God that is within you." The Principle becomes manifestation so that manifestation might rebecome the Principle,[1] or so that the "I" might return to the Self; or simply, so that the human soul might, through given phenomena, make contact with

---

1. Saint Irenaeus: "God became man that man might become God."

the heavenly archetypes, and thereby with its own archetype.

In our vital experiences and in our artistic productions, the influx of the celestial Benediction is conditional upon the sacrificial element; on the contrary, in totally naturalistic art — since it exhausts the creative trajectory — nothing spiritual is left, nothing sacred, hence no longer any radiation. It is true that a naturalistic work may have an interiorizing effect through its content, but in this case it is the model that has this effect and not the work as such; the naturalistic contradiction between the appearance of life and inert matter can only harm the message.

But there is something else: the notion of naturalism is rather loose because it expresses not only an excess but also a tendency that is legitimate and on the whole logical: when a work imitates nature by observing certain principles, that is, by insisting upon what is essential and not what is merely accidental,[2] it may be called naturalistic without this term having to evoke the faults of total naturalism. The work of art is then valid, not because it copies nature, but because it does so in a certain manner: because it translates what is perceived into a new language which, in addition, makes explicit the profound intention of things, and this means that the work must present itself as a human production and not merely as an imitation of nature.

*
* *

Independently of any question of naturalism, it frequently happens in modern art — as in literature — that the author wishes to say too much: exteriorization is pushed too far, as if nothing should remain within. This tendency appears in all modern arts, including poetry and music;

---

2. In addition, the work ought to conform to the material utilized by the artist, and also — in the case of painting — to the rules required by the flat surface, and other conditions of the kind.

here again, what is lacking is the instinct of sacrifice, sobriety, restraint; the creator completely empties himself, and in so doing, he invites others to empty themselves as well and thereby to lose all the essential, namely the taste for the secret and the sense of inwardness, whereas the work's reason for being is contemplative and unitive interiorization.

Without wishing to be too systematic, it can be said that with most traditional artists, it is the element "object" that determines the work; with the majority of modern artists on the contrary, it is the element "subject," in the sense that the moderns — individualistic as they are — intend to "create" the work and in creating it, wish to express their altogether profane little personality; whence ambition and the pursuit of originality. To be sure, the non-modern artist also, and by the nature of things, inevitably expresses his personality; but he does so through the object and by his quest of the object. Conversely, the modern artist — we mean "modernistic" — is necessarily preoccupied with the object, but within the framework and in the interest of his subjectivism;[3] the apprentice artist no longer has to learn to draw, he has to learn to "create"; it is the world turned upside down.

It is significant that in extra-traditional art[4] valid works — which may be masterpieces — are necessarily accompanied by a flood of meaningless or subversive productions, and these often by one and the same author; this is the ransom of an excess of liberty, or let us say of an absence of truth, of piety, of discipline based on spiritual foundations.

---

3. Let us note that originally, the word "subject" was a synonym for "predicate" and also for "substance"; it is only with Kant that the "subject" became the conscious, the knower and the thinker. But as this interpretation has become common in modern language, we follow its usage.

4. We are not speaking of ultra-modern pseudo-art, which for us does not exist.

Unquestionably, this is the drama of all modern "culture" and has been so since its beginnings; and let us add that this culture ends by destroying itself, precisely owing to the contradiction between the rights it claims and the duties it ignores. Semitic iconophobia seems to be aware of this implicitly, even though its principal motivation is the danger of idolatry; this danger, in any case, contains in a certain manner and secondarily that of the cult of "genius" and of "culture."

*
* *

It is necessary to distinguish between an idolatry that is objective and another that is subjective: in the first case, it is the image itself that is erroneous, because it is supposed to be a god; in the second case, the image may pertain to sacred art and it is the lack of contemplativity that constitutes idolatry; it is because man no longer knows how to perceive the metaphysical transparency of phenomena, images and symbols that he is idolatrous.

Grosso modo, the Aryans and the Mongols are iconophilic; the Semites and Semiticized peoples are iconophobic. The conflict between the iconodules and the iconoclasts of the early Church is explained by the fact that a Semitic religion was superimposed on an Aryan mentality; thus it was necessary to make a choice, and the Aryan spirit prevailed in the end. Protestant iconoclasm was independent of the question of mentality; it is to be explained solely by the return to Scripture, which de facto is Semitic.

If in the early Church it was the icons that won the case, it was obviously so — as in the case of alimentary prescriptions — because the right solution imposed itself thanks to a revelation: it was Saint Luke, an apostle, who created the first icon of the Virgin; and it was Saint Veronica, with the Holy Shroud, who was at the origin of the image of the Holy Face. The very principle of the "sacred portrait" is expressed in this Buddhist saying: "The Buddhas also save by their superhuman beauty." But not only is there the iconophobia of the Semites of nomadic origin, there is also the absence of images among most of the shamanistic Mongol peoples, notably the Red Indians; in this case, the divine image is absent, not because of a theological principle concerned with preventing given abuses, but because virgin Nature is itself "divine image"; because it is for the Great Spirit, and not for man, to furnish the image-sacrament of the Invisible.

As regards sacred art, it must be said that painted and sculpted images also have God as their author since it is He who reveals and creates them through man; He offers the image of Himself by humanizing it, for if man is "made in God's image," it is because God is the prototype of the human image. If virgin Nature is the image of God, then man, who is situated at the center of this Nature is so as well; on the one hand, he is witness to the Divine image that surrounds him, and on the other hand, he is himself this image when God, in sacred art, takes on the form of man.

It is clearly the deiformity of the human body that has inspired sacred nudity; discredited in the Semitic religions for reasons of spiritual perspective and social opportuneness — although it has been manifested sporadically among contemplatives disposed to primordiality — it is still the order of the day in India, immemorial homeland of the "gymnosophists." Krishna, in removing all clothing from the adoring gopis, "baptized" them so to speak: he reduced them to the state before the "fall."[5] The path of liberation is to rebecome what one is.

5. In the climate of Semitic monotheism, dress doubtless represents the choice of the "spirit" against the "flesh"; nonetheless the body intrinsically expresses deiformity, hence primordial "divinity" and immanence. In a certain sense, if dress indicates the soul or the function, the body indicates the Intellect.

The Spiritual Meaning of Work

The modern cult of work is founded on the one hand on the fact that work is a necessity for the majority of men, and on the other hand on the human tendency to make a virtue of an unavoidable constraint. The Bible, however, presents work as a sort of punishment: "In the sweat of thy face shalt thou eat bread"; prior to the original sin and the Fall, the first human pair knew no work. There have always and everywhere been contemplative saints who — without thereby being lazy — have not worked, and all the traditional worlds afford — or did afford — the sight of beggars to whom alms are given without anything being asked of them, except perhaps prayers; no Hindu would dream of blaming a Ramakrishna or a Ramana Maharshi for the fact that he did not engage in any profession. It is generalized impiety, the suppression of the sacred in public life and the constraints of industrialism that have had the effect of making work a "categorical imperative" outside which — it is believed — there is only culpable laziness and corruption.

Be that as it may, there is work and then there is work: there has always been noble agriculture as well as crafts plied at home or in the workshops of the former guilds; and then, since the nineteenth century, there has been industrial servitude in factories; a servitude all the more brutalizing, if not degrading, in that its object is the machine, and that most of the time it offers no properly human satisfaction to the workman. Nevertheless, even this work — in general more quantitative than qualitative — can subjectively have a sacred or sanctifying character thanks to the spiritual attitude of the worker if, knowing that he cannot change the world and that he must earn a living for himself and his family, he strives, according to the possibilities available to him, to combine his work with consciousness of our final ends and the "remembrance of God"; *ora et labora.*

This having been said, it should be added that freedom consists much more in satisfaction with our particular situation than in the total absence of constraints, an absence scarcely realizable in the here-below, and which moreover is not always a guarantee of happiness.

*

* *

The great spiritual methods, even those which insist the most expressly on the excellence of the eremitical life, have never excluded the possibility of following a path in the midst of the occupations of life in the world; the example of the Third Orders is proof of this. The question we propose to answer here is that of knowing how it is possible to reconcile an intense spiritual life with the obligations of outward life, and even to integrate those obligations into the inward life; for if one's daily work — whether one's profession or housework — does not constitute an obstacle to the spiritual path, this implies that it should play the role of a positive element in it, or more precisely the role of a secondary support for the realization of the Divine within us.

Such an integration of work into spirituality depends on three fundamental conditions which we shall designate respectively by the terms "necessity," "sanctification" and "perfection." The first of these conditions implies that the activity to be spiritualized correspond to a necessity and not to a mere whim: one can sanctify — or offer to God — any normal activity necessitated by the requirements of life itself, but not just any pastime lacking a sufficient reason or having a reprehensible character. This amounts to saying that any necessary activity possesses a character that predisposes it to conveying the spirit; all necessary activities in fact have a certain universality which renders them eminently symbolic.

The second of the three conditions implies that the activity thus defined be actually offered to God, which is to say that it be done through love of God and without rebelling against destiny; this is the meaning of the prayers by which — in most if not all traditional forms — work is consecrated, and thus ritualized, meaning that it becomes a "natural sacrament," a kind of shadow or secondary counterpart of the "supernatural sacrament" that is the rite properly speaking.

Finally, the third condition implies the logical perfection of the work, for it is evident that one cannot offer an imperfect thing to God, nor consecrate a base object to Him; moreover, the perfection of the act is as self-evident as that of existence itself, in the sense that every act is supposed to retrace the Divine Act and at the same time a modality of it. This perfection of action comprises three aspects, which refer respectively to the activity as such, then to the means and finally to the purpose; in other words, the activity as such ought to be objectively and subjectively perfect, which implies that it be conformable or proportionate to the end to be attained; the means should also be conformable and proportionate to the goal envisioned, which implies that the instrument of the work be well chosen, then wielded with skill, which is to say in perfect conformity with the nature of the work; finally, the result of the work has to be perfect, and must answer exactly to the need from which it has arisen.

If these conditions, which constitute what could be called the internal and external "logic" of the activity, are properly fulfilled, the work not only will no longer be an obstacle to the inward path, it will even be a help. Conversely, work poorly done will always be an impediment to the path, because it does not correspond to any Divine Possibility; God is Perfection, and man — in order to approach God — must be perfect in action as well as in non-active contemplation.

Part Two

Man, Truth and the Path

Faculties and Modalities of Man

Man's fundamental faculties are Intelligence, Will and Sentiment; this last word taken in its deepest sense. We could also say, from a certain point of view: Knowledge, Fear and Love; and by analogy: Essence, Rigor and Mildness. Understanding through Intelligence that above us and within us there is the absolutely Real and the Sovereign Good — the Real by which we exist and the Good from which stems all that makes us happy — we cannot, in good logic, not wish to attain to this Real which is the Good; and that which we wish to attain a posteriori through Will and work, we must realize a priori through Love and virtue, *Deo juvante.*

Intelligence, Will, Sentiment. Man possesses in addition four instrumental faculties, namely: Reason, which is objective and discriminative; Desire, which is subjective and unifying; Imagination, which is active and creative; Memory, which is passive and conservative. Reason is not Intelligence in itself, it is only its instrument, and this on the express condition that it be inspired by intellectual Intuition, or simply correct ideas or exact facts; nothing is worse than the mind cut off from its root; *corruptio optimi pessima.* The Intellect — *aliquid increatum et increabile* — dominates and ennobles our fundamental faculties: it is by it that our Reason exists and that it is objective and total; and again it is by it that our Will is free, hence capable of moral heroism,

and that our Sentiment is disinterested, hence capable of
compassion and generosity.

Reason is the proof of the divine spark that dwells in the
depths of the human heart, and without which man himself
would have no meaning, he who is "made in the image of
God."

*

* *

In addition to the fundamental and instrumental — or
"cardiac" and "mental" — faculties that all men have in
common, there are modalities which on the contrary differ-
entiate them. Thus it is necessary to distinguish between
virtues and talents: the former are "celestial" and "vertical," and the latter, "terrestrial" and "horizontal"; which
means that the former are intrinsically necessary whereas
the latter are simply useful, at least in a spiritual context. A
man may be a saint without being a genius, and a genius
without being a saint; but in men of a prophetic nature both
values are necessarily combined to the extent that they have
a creative mission.

Other human modalities are the various temperaments
and characters: namely, Activity, Passivity, Lightness, Heavi-
ness, Indifferentiation; or symbolically speaking: fire, water,
air, earth, ether; or again, in other words: discriminative
combativeness, contemplative quietude, holy carefreeness,
holy gravity, then their common intention. Accentuations
of character are assuredly legitimate on condition that they
be in accordance with an equilibrium that summarizes
them and gives to each its due.

*

* *

For some, the starting point of the Path is the conviction
that man is fundamentally corrupted, hence that he is
intrinsically a sinner and that he is in need of a Messiah to
save him; for others, the starting point is on the contrary

the very nature of man — total Intelligence, free Will, compassionate Character — on condition that it be turned to account by Revelation and Intellection, and by the means of grace that proceed from it.[1]

Clearly, both these ways of approach can be combined, given that the profound and normative potentials of man are everywhere and always the same; there is no scission in our deiform nature.

*
* *

Virtue is in man's nature because it is in the logic of things; man being "made in the image of God." It is this man we have in mind, and not his nature disfigured by the cosmic fatality of which the Bible offers a symbolist account. Where there is virtue, there is grace; the angels confer grace upon virtue as wine is poured into a cup of crystal or gold. Man's deiformity appears a priori in the vertical posture of his body and in the gift of speech: verticality obligates to the dignity of *pontifex* which it manifests, and speech obligates to truth and to communication of the good, starting with the celestial Message hidden in the heart.

In summary, there is but one sole virtue, the love of God and the neighbor; however, it is diversified owing to the complexity of the human soul and earthly situations. Yet there is more: the moral qualities mutually perfect and enhance one another: thus patience is perfect only with the concurrence of trust, which adds to it an element of gentleness; conversely, trust demands a complement of rigor, and this is patience, precisely. Perfection lies in the equilibrium between complementary opposites.

---

1. Both perspectives are reflected in the distinction made by the Japanese Amidists between "Other-power" *(tariki)* and "Self-power" *(jiriki);* in fact, neither of the two ways can exclude the other altogether, for one always has need, on the one hand of a certain intelligence, and on the other of a certain grace.

In an analogous way, the quality of fervor is perfect only when accompanied by the quality of contentment that confers upon it a perfume of serenity, and contentment in its turn is all the more well-rooted when it is allied to fervor.

Similarly again: the virtue of humility is deepened thanks to its alliance with the virtue of dignity, of the consciousness of the "Motionless Mover" in which we participate by our deiformity; conversely, there is no wholesome dignity without the quality of humility.

Finally, the virtue of charity should be accompanied by the virtue of justice, hence of the sense of duties and rights, for goodness cannot have precedence over truth; conversely, the rigor of justice will be compensated by the mildness of charity, for "love thy neighbor as thyself."

*
*   *

A man's personality is derived essentially from an idea, or more exactly from a set of ideas grouped around a central and determining idea. From these ideas are derived behaviors that manifest them and put them into practice; for man, who is an active being, ideas essentially entail consequences. It is this that determines the personality, leaving aside subjective factors such as tendencies and qualifications, which confer upon the personality its form or its style. In any case, a personality cannot be extracted from the void, and besides, it has no meaning apart from its fundamental contents; the modern mania for "finding one's personality" is a perversion pure and simple; it is "putting the cart before the horse." The first condition of a legitimate personality is not to desire to have one; we ought to want to be that which is, and not that which is not.

No doubt, experiences contribute to forming the personality; to giving it a form, but not a substance, for the substance depends upon the Truth and not upon given accidents. Experiences can help us to become what we ought to be, that is, precisely, to disengage our true personality, which could only be a reflection — or a prolongation — of the principial and celestial Personality, the only one that is. Let no one say "this is what I am, you have to take me as I am"; for we are nothing outside the Will of God.

*

* *

The two great pitfalls of earthly life are outwardness and matter; or more exactly disproportionate outwardness and corruptible matter. Outwardness is the lack of equilibrium between our tendency towards outward things and our tendency towards the inward, the "kingdom of God"; and matter is the lower substance — lower in relation to our spiritual nature — in which we are imprisoned on earth.

What is imperative is, not to reject the outward by allowing only the inward, but to realize a relationship with the inward — a spiritual inwardness, precisely — which removes from outwardness its tyranny at once dispersing and compressing, and which allows us to "see God everywhere"; that is, to perceive archetypes and symbols in things, in short, to integrate the outward into the inward and to make of it a support for inwardness. Beauty, perceived by a spiritually interiorized soul, is interiorizing; a prideful or narcissistic inwardness must not be confused with holy inwardness.

And as regards matter: what is imperative is not to deny it — if this were possible — but to remove its seductive tyranny; to distinguish in it what is archetypal and pure from what is accidental and impure; to treat it with nobleness and sobriety. "Unto the pure all things are pure."

*

* *

Man's reason for being is the Consciousness which the divine Self has of Itself, and which must reverberate within

61

Contingency in virtue of the Infinitude of the Divine Principle.

Our relationship with the world is something conditional, relative; our relationship with Heaven on the contrary is something unconditional and imprescriptible. The only thing that counts absolutely is our consciousness of the Absolute; all the rest is in God's hands.

Axioms of the *Sophia Perennis*

There are truths which are axioms because they are self-evident, and which therefore can be proven *ab extra;* there are others which are axiomatic because they are present in the very substance of the intelligence, so that, *ipso facto,* their evidence can only be attested to *ab intra;* and this raises the question of knowing what is meant by a proof. We would say that verification *ab intra* is quasi-existential: certain conditions must have been realized to be able to perceive that which is to be proven, if this word has a meaning here. However, the fact that metaphysical axioms are verified "from within" could not mean they cannot be "illustrated" *ab extra* and by the use of reason; for reasonings can perfectly well offer keys to direct intellection, otherwise there would be no books nor any doctrines; as for receptivity with regard to rationally graspable arguments, everything depends on our fundamental tendencies, namely on the question of knowing, not what we think, but what we are.

*

* *

We say that there is an absolute, transcendent Reality, unperceivable by the senses, beyond space and time; but knowable by the pure Intellect, by which It makes Itself present; a Reality which, without ever undergoing the

63

least change since It is unconditional, gives rise — by virtue of Its very Infinitude — to a dimension of contingency or relativity in order to be able to realize the mystery of Its radiation. For "it is in the nature of the Good to wish to communicate Itself": this means that God wishes to be known not only in Himself, but also "from without" and starting from an "other than He"; that is the very substance of the Divine All-Possibility.

This is what we say, or recall, a priori. We say it, not only because we believe it, but because we know it, and we know it because we are it. We are it in our transpersonal Intellect, which intrinsically is the vehicle of the immanent Presence of the Absolute Real, and without which we would not be men.

*

* *

Thus human intelligence — by the fact that it is capable of essentiality and totality — contains in its substance the fundamental data of the *Sophia Perennis,* namely: absolute Reality which by definition is the Sovereign Good; then its Infinitude — All-Possibility — which is its intrinsic consequence and which causes that projection which is Relativity or Contingency. The Relative on the one hand is prefigured in the Absolute-Infinite and on the other hand manifests the latter at various degrees; now the cosmogonical projection, since it necessarily moves away from the Principle, just as necessarily gives rise, within Manifestation which it creates, to the enigma that is imperfection, privation, absurdity, evil; but evil, being quite paradoxically the image of a naught inexistent in itself, cannot prevail against the Good which is the very essence of Being; *vincit omnia Veritas.*

At a doubtless more elementary but nevertheless essential level, our spirit contains the following axioms: there is

a God, all-powerful and a priori fundamentally benevo-
lent;[1] He is our Benefactor and will be our Judge; our soul
is immortal; it has the twofold vocation of prayer and virtue;
it is made for Salvation and Beatitude. This is our innate
theology, whether we like it or not;[2] and "blessed are they
who have not seen and yet have believed."

*

*   *

The fact that the Principle and Manifestation are incom-
mensurable could not mean that they are totally foreign to
each other; quite the contrary, Manifestation is necessarily
prefigured in the principial order, which for its part is just
as necessarily reflected in the manifested order; the world
contains modes of the divine Presence, just as the divine
Intellect contains the prototypes of the phenomena of the
world; in other words, God is present in the world through
sacred things, and the world is present in God through the
Platonic Ideas.

On the one hand, Manifestation is positive since it
expresses the Principle, but on the other hand, it has a
negative character in that it inevitably moves away from the
Principle and thereby opposes It. Despite this ambiguity, it
is positive in itself, precisely because its reason for being is
to bring about the radiation of the Divine Sun, which allows
us to say that it is more truly a good which comprises some
evils, rather than an evil which comprises some good. This
preponderance of the positive aspect is explained by the
very nature of Being, which by definition is the *Agathón,* the

1. "God alone is good," according to the Gospels. According to the
Koran, "My Mercy precedeth *(sabaqat)* my Wrath"; the meaning of the
verb is principial, not only temporal; "Mercy" *(Raḥmah)* is intrinsic, and
"Wrath" *(Ghadab)* extrinsic.
2. This is why there is no people without religion, which "illustrates"
in its manner our thesis of the immanence of spiritual notions.

supreme Good, and *ipso facto* the archetype and source of all possible good. Quite evidently, privation is the accident while value is the substance; the Universe could not possibly begin with a privation; if Being did not coincide with the Good, there would be no good whatsoever in the world. We insist on all these data — at the risk of being repetitive — because of their at once subtle and fundamental character.

According to Plato and Saint Augustine, the cause of the world is the tendency of the Good to communicate Itself; negatively speaking, this cause is a result of the Infinitude of the Supreme Principle, which necessarily implies the "possibility of the impossible," namely the possibility of the Absolute not to be the Absolute. But since this possibility is absurd, it can be realized only in an illusory dimension, that of Relativity, of *Māyā;* whence the ambiguous possibility of the world, precisely.

*

*   *

Philosophically speaking, there are two great problems, that of Being, of Reality, and that of Consciousness or of Knowledge; these are problems because of the prejudice which treats the roots of Existence as if sensible objects were in question. For the gnostic — for the born metaphysician — there are no problems; he perceives Being — or conceives of It — through phenomena, and perceiving Being, he knows *ipso facto* that he "is" what he "knows."[3]

The sufficient reason for human intelligence — but for which man would not exist — is that which it alone is capable of attaining to. We are made in order to be the mirror of the absolutely Real, that is to say in order to know

---

3. "*Brahma* is Truth *(Satyam)*, the world is appearance *(mithyā);* the soul is not different from *Brahma.*"

the Absolute starting from Relativity; and this is so in virtue of the illimitation of the divine Possibility which could not exclude this indirect way of Consciousness of the Self. Now to know total Reality is to know it totally; it follows that man must know with all his being: he must will what he knows and love what he knows and wills, given that the supreme Object of his knowledge is the Absolute, precisely. The certainty of the knowledge of the Absolute is absolute, for it coincides with That which is.

The Mystery of Possibility

"God doeth what He willeth": which means, not that God, like an individual, can have arbitrary desires, but that pure Being by its very nature comprises All-Possibility. Now the limitlessness of the latter implies possibilities which are so to speak absurd, namely contrary to the nature of Being, a nature that every phenomenon is after all supposed to manifest, and does manifest whether it would or not; these possibilities clearly can be realized only in an illusory and delimited mode, since no evil can penetrate into the celestial order. Evil, far from constituting half of the possible — for there is no symmetry between good and evil — is limited by space and time to the point of being reduced to a minute quantity in the economy of the total Universe; it is necessarily so since "Mercy embraceth all things."

In other words: the Divine Infinitude entails that the Supreme Principle consent, not only to limiting Itself ontologically — by degrees and in view of universal Manifestation — but also to allowing Itself to be contradicted within the latter; every metaphysician admits this intellectually, but it is far from being the case that everyone is able to accept it morally, namely to be resigned to the concrete consequences of the principle of necessary absurdity.

*

* *

In order to resolve the thorny problem of evil, some have claimed that nothing is bad since everything which happens is "willed by God," or that evil exists only "from the standpoint of the Law"; which is by no means plausible, first because it is God who promulgates the Law, and then because the Law exists on account of evil and not conversely. What should be said is that evil is integrated into the universal Good, not as evil but as an ontological necessity, as we have pointed out above; this necessity underlies evil, it is metaphysically inherent in it, without however transforming it into a good.

Thus it should not be said that God "wills" evil — we say rather that He "permits" it — nor that evil is a good because God is not opposed to its existence; on the other hand, it may be said that we must accept the "will of God" when evil enters into our destiny and we are unable to escape it, or for as long as we are unable to do so. Moreover, let us not lose sight of the fact that the complement of resignation is trust, whose quintessence is the certitude at once metaphysical and eschatological that we bear deep within ourselves; unconditional certitude of That which is, and conditional certitude of that which we can be.

The Ternary Rhythm of the Spirit

Existence can be compared to a dilation starting from a point. To say dilation, is to say cycle: that which "goes out" will have to "come back"; that which increases will decrease. There is Existence and "existences": it has been said of Existence that it is without beginning and without end, which means basically that it constitutes a necessary dimension of Divine Reality, and is consequently "permanent" according to this relationship, without however escaping the law of cyclic coming-and-going; but existences, for their part, blossom and disappear so to speak before our very eyes, and we cannot doubt that the visible universe surrounding us will be called to disappear in its turn.

Death is the passage through the point from which our earthly deployment has come forth. On the spiritual plane, "to die before dying," is to realize consciously and willingly what the dying man experiences involuntarily; it is never to lose sight of the point whence we have issued, namely pure Existence.

Three poles can be discerned in the total Universe: "Being," "Consciousness," "Joy"; this is the well known Vedantic ternary. Being and Consciousness are the roots of the Universe; Joy deploys the Universe in carrying the other two elements to the confines of Manifestation. Sanctity, or wisdom, has an existential or ontological pole and an intellectual pole: according to the first relationship, the soul "remains what it is," it reposes in its initial simplicity, in its primary innocence; it remains conscious of its substance and does not squander itself in phenomena. This is what could be called, in Christian terms, the "Marian mystery"; it is "childlikeness," "poverty," "humility." The tangible expressions of this perfection are the virtues; but it is also expressed by beauty, at all the degrees of creation, and in art as well as in nature. Beauty does not wish to conquer anything, it always reposes in "That which is"; like the love of which Saint Paul speaks, it "seeketh not her own, is not easily provoked." To be wise or holy, is to one degree or another to remain "that which God has made us."

According to the relationship of the element "Consciousness" or "Intelligence," the sage realizes a return to the quintessence in an analogous manner: his mind is concentrated, it maintains itself in the transpersonal climate of the Intellect; it does not lose itself in "what is thought," but tends to identify with "That which thinks," with the Intellect itself. The mind, rather than reposing in its being, is concentrated on its essence; but quite evidently the one does not go without the other. What the virtues are to existential perfection, truths are to intellectual perfection; virtue is essentially simplicity, inward beauty, generosity, whereas truth, for its part, lies entirely in the discernment between the Real and the illusory or between the Absolute and the contingent. To say that the intelligence lies in truth, that it is thus consistent with its own nature, means first of all that its objective content is the Real with all its ramifications, and then that it concentrates on its own essence; and to say that the will lies in virtue means first of all that it is directed outwardly according to the laws of beauty and goodness, and then that it reposes inwardly in its own nature, in pure Existence.

Man is created by Joy and he lives from it; but since he is fallen, his happiness tends towards idolatry; joy — which is holy and pure with God — deviates with man to the extent that it usurps the place of the spiritual and becomes an end in itself, a luciferian and impure cult. In order to reintegrate human joy into universal Joy, its movement must be reversed: one must place one's happiness in the two preceding movements, existential simplicity and intellectual consciousness; one must be "harmless as doves and wise as serpents" and, knowing that the "kingdom of Heaven is within you," not seek happiness in phenomena. Heaven in its Mercy comes to meet our weakness of seeking happiness outside ourselves: it offers to our joy an object that exteriorizes our inwardness and reabsorbs the centrifugal impulses of joy, and this is the Symbol, which is essentially the "manifestation of the unmanifest" or "form of the formless."[1] All functions which are natural and consecrated by divine Law are attached to the element Symbol and are like its emanations; the Symbol is everywhere, as God is everywhere; things become transparent in virtue of their symbolism. But if the element joy can be tapped and canalized in various ways in view of God, the fundamental movement of joy must be directed towards the contemplation of God in pure Existence and in pure Intelligence; only this contemplation, or this effort of contemplation — in its elementary forms of virtue and faith — can allow for the integration of "sensible consolations" into supernatural Joy; it is only through this effort and through this integration that pleasure is worthy of man, and that man is worthy of Grace. We must place our happiness in what we are, not in what we desire; man must seek his happiness above himself, and thus find it within himself.

*
* *

1. In other words: the Symbol is an "exteriorization in view of an interiorization," and this is evinced in a particularly striking way in Buddhist art where the images express, with a sometimes unsurpassable power, all the transcendent serenity of the Blessed One.

The revealed Symbol is an objectification of Truth and Beauty, or of Knowledge and Virtue; it objectifies the poles "Consciousness" and "Being," and likewise — and through its very manifestation — the pole "Joy." Through the Symbol, our joy or our love is placed virtually in Consciousness and Being and "is transported upstream" to Beatitude.

God is Being, Consciousness and Beatitude; it is the latter that carries the elements Being and Consciousness to the confines of Manifestation, which is to say that it deploys the world by means of these two elements; it is by this "divine movement" that Existence and Intelligence are affirmed everywhere, it is this movement that projects "in the direction of nothingness" the myriades of existing, conscious and acting creatures, which multiply and spread in their turn. This divine movement goes from Being to "nothingness" and from "nothingness" to Being: God creates man, but man, who cannot realize the creation and who figures in it as a mirror of the Creator, must realize God starting from "nothingness"; man's end is in the conscious and free reflux towards the divine Being.

An Enigma of the Gospel

In speaking of the Last Supper, the Gospel relates an enigmatic and even disturbing incident: Christ gives Judas a sop of bread to eat and tells him, "That thou doest, do quickly"; and at that moment, Satan enters into Judas, who then leaves the room. This gives the impression that Christ took upon himself the responsibility for the betrayal, *quod absit*.

The explanation of the enigma is as follows: nothing can happen counter to the Will of God; the fact that something happens means that God has "willed" it. Now God cannot expressly will a particular evil, but He must tolerate in a certain fashion evil as such, since this is included in the — partly paradoxical — limitlessness of the Divine All-Possibility. For this reason, God cannot not allow some particular evil, but it should be said that He "permits" it and not that He "wills" it; and He permits it, not inasmuch as it is an evil, but inasmuch as it is an indirect and inevitable contribution to a good. Christ willed, certainly not the betrayal in itself, but the Redemption.[1]

It remains to be known why Christ acted as mentioned above, for his acceptance of the evil could have been silent; now it could have been so in principle, but not in fact, and that is the root of the problem. It was necessary to show the

1. Let us recall here that Saint Augustine, speaking of the sin of Adam and Eve, exclaimed: *"felix culpa!"* since, he thought, this sin was the cause of the Redemption.

world that the devil has no power over God, that he can only apparently oppose God and thanks to a Divine Will; that nothing can be done outside the Will of the Sovereign Good; that if the powers of evil oppose — or believe they can oppose — the Divinity, this can only be in virtue of a Divine decision; whence the injunction "That thou doest, do quickly." Thus, the devil does not even have the power to betray without a Divine causation, metaphysically speaking; in the Gospel account, this power escapes him, therefore he could not triumph. And if, in this account, the devil enters into Judas, that is because he obtained the freedom to do so — a subtle entanglement of causes, but ontologically plausible. What is ill-sounding in the salvific drama of Christianity is that the Redemption seems to depend on a traitor; it was necessary to deprive the adversary of this satisfaction.

Be that as it may, the fact that Christianity had need of Judas implies — and this seems to be the height of paradox — that this traitor could not be a fundamentally bad man, as the popular belief would have it; and in fact, he was not, as is proven by his repentance and his despair.[2] Neither were the other two accused, Caiphas and Pilate, as black as they are painted; for the former, the extenuating circumstance was his orthodoxy, and for the latter, his good will. We would even go so far as to say that their necessary cooperation in the Redemption implies that in the final analysis all three were forgiven; only this conclusion, so it seems to us, can protect Christianity from the possible blame for depending upon criminal causes and, so to speak, for being founded upon them. And we think here of this prayer of Christ: "Father, forgive them, for they know not what they do"; now it is impossible to assume, in good logic, that a prayer of Christ would not have been granted.

---

2. If Judas had been what is thought, he would on the contrary have been proud of his crime. At the very moment of the betrayal, Jesus called him "my friend"; in this expression there was perhaps a glimmer of the Divine pardon.

It would have been a kind of victory if the Church had instituted a feast of the three great Pardons, but it could not — for moral reasons — "allow itself this luxury," because it would have given *carte blanche* to all evildoers; de facto, not de jure, of course. It is for this reason that Christ had to say, speaking of Judas, that "it had been good for that man if he had not been born"; this does not mean that Judas is in the eternal hell that Christian theology imagines, but it may mean that Judas, while not being damned, must remain in purgatory until the end of the world.

Caiphas could be blamed for not having been sensitive to the divine nature of Christ, but besides his Mosaic orthodoxy, he had also as an extenuating circumstance the fact that Christ was never concerned with making himself understood. In addition, Christ was not interested in the "prescriptions of men," even if they were plausible; what mattered to him was solely the sincerity of our love for God. This is not exactly the perspective of Moses, and the Pharisees cannot be blamed for not adhering to it at the level that was theirs, any more than one can blame the authorities of Brahmanism for not having converted to the Buddha's perspective.

It could be argued that the Jews have had to suffer as heirs of Judas and Caiphas, but it could as well be argued that the Christians as heirs of Pilate[3] — through the Renaissance — have had, and still have, to suffer by undergoing the consequences of the "humanist" but finally inhuman world they created at the time of the Borgias and which they continue to create in our day;[4] unquestionably, the Renaissance was a betrayal, although it also comprised

3. That is to say that Pilate was the representative of Tiberius, of whom Charlemagne as well as Constantine were the heirs; it is worth noting that for the Moslem, the Christian is *"rūmī,"* that is, "Roman."
4. It could be objected that the Eastern Church was not responsible for the Renaissance, which is true, but the Orthodox countries were dragged into its orbit by Peter the Great. In fact, Eastern Europe is part

some positive elements, which however could not compensate for its comprehensive error.

In order to understand Christ's attitude towards "the scribes and the pharisees," one has to keep in mind the following: at that time, Judaism was undergoing a phase of "ossification" comparable to that of Brahmanism at the time of the Buddha, and this was providential in both cases. The history of mankind is a *līlā*, a "divine play": possibilities in turn have to manifest and exhaust themselves. Be that as it may, Caiphas and his partisans can be blamed for not wanting to acknowledge the decadence of their surroundings which was incontestable, otherwise Christ would not have stigmatized it; and it is certainly not for the first time in the history of Israel that a prophet hurls thunderbolts at a corrupted and hypocritical clergy.

Like Al-Hallaj — that "Christly" manifestation in the midst of Islam — Christ manifested his celestial nature without being concerned with making it intelligible; he incarnated his destiny and he wished to be that which he had to be in the economy of religious and mystical possibilities. A founder of religion personifies a spiritual perspective and a path of salvation; he expresses himself in a direct and quasi-absolute fashion and need not make the commentaries which theologians and wise men will make later.

"And the light shineth in the darkness, and the darkness comprehended it not." This concerns not only the Jews and the pagans, but also the Christians, as history proves.[5] Christ, like Moses, put God above man; the Renaissance, like Tiberius, put man in the place of God; whereas Christ had said: "Thy kingdom come!"

---

of the modern world, mentally as well as materially; Greece was speedily brought to heel after the departure of the Turks.

5. Let us remark that there are orthodox Jews who, while rejecting Christianity, and in flagrant opposition to the Talmud, admit that Jesus was a misunderstood prophet, of Eliatic and Essenian type.

Characteristics of
Voluntaristic Mysticism

Voluntaristic mysticism is a path of love which — in contrast with Hindu *bhakti* — is characterized by the fact that no intellectual element intervenes in an active fashion in its method; also the qualifications it demands are almost exclusively moral: at most it demands a general predisposition which, together with moral factors and on contact with grace, becomes a "vocation." It is true that this mysticism thrives on dogmatic symbols and theological concepts, but not on intellections: it is entirely centered on love — on the will with its emotive concomitances — and not on gnosis. In a certain sense, voluntaristic mysticism is "negative," since its method — apart from sacramental graces — consists above all in the negation of the natural appetites, whence the cult of suffering and the importance of trials and consolations; the activity is purely moral and ascetic, as the following opinion of Saint John of the Cross shows well: "By its nature, this [our mind] is limited to natural science; but God has nevertheless endowed it with an obediential power in regard to the supernatural, so that it can obey whenever it pleases Our Lord to make it act supernaturally. Strictly speaking, no knowledge is accessible to the mind except by natural means; therefore all knowledge must pass through the senses" *(The Ascent of Mount Carmel, I, 2)*. This is the negation of the intellect, the reduction of the intelligence to reason alone. In such a perspective, there is no place for the intellective man; there is no path for him. The consequence is that he is condemned to occupy himself with philosophy; given his need for logic and the nature of his aspiration, he cannot follow the path of love — the only one offered to him — except on the margin; his particular vocation falls so to speak into the void.

An especially striking characteristic of voluntaristic mysticism is sentimental humility, which appears as an end in itself and which excludes all help from the intelligence. Humility as such is certainly everywhere a condition of spirituality, but it is only in "passional" mysticism that it is situated on the plane of sentimentality, which proves that the human groups to whom it is addressed have a fundamental tendency to the sort of obsession with the ego that is individualism; this obsession or this "pride" has an influence on the intelligence, whence the propensity to Promethean thought, to rationalism, to philosophical adventures, to the divinization of passional art, to egocentricity in all its forms. In human groups whose mentality is not centered on the individual and on the individual point of view, asceticism could not put the emphasis on a systematic and blind humiliation that is contrary to the nature of things and also to the intelligence. If we divide men into two groups, contemplatives and those whose natural vocation lies in action, we could say that the first are much less obsessed with the ego than the second, and even that the passional element in them has something quasi-impersonal about it, in the sense that their passion is much more passion as such than that of a particular ego; it hardly encroaches on their intelligence, especially since the latter determines passion and not conversely. What perhaps most distinguishes the born metaphysician from the ordinary man is that in the former, passion stops where intelligence begins, whereas in the latter, the intelligence does not by itself oppose the passional element, of which it readily becomes the vehicle. By the way, it is important to know that anti-intellectual mysticism is not an exclusively Christian phenomenon; it is also to be found in the two other monotheistic religions and even, incidentally, in Hindu bhaktism.

*

* *

Sentimental humility seeks out pride because it has need of it, and is fundamentally suspicious of any perspective that transcends the moral alternative on which it lives, and this explains the sacrifice of the intelligence in the name of Virtue. Saint Theresa of Avila, whose intelligence was keen, had no difficulty in recognizing the dangers of this position, but she did not find any decisive remedy for it, given the empirical character of her own point of view. She did not wish to remain "sunk in the consideration of our own misery," and she believed that: "never will the stream of our works come out clean and pure from the mud of fear, weakness, cowardice, and a thousand troublesome thoughts, such as these: are not people looking at me? In taking this road, am I not going to be led astray? Is it not presumption to dare undertake this good work? Is it not pride, is it not worse still, that a creature like me should occupy herself with a matter as lofty as prayer? Will people not have too good an opinion of me if I abandon the common and ordinary way? Must one not avoid all excess, even in virtue? Sinner that I am, will the wish to raise myself not simply expose myself to the risk of falling from higher up? Perhaps I shall stop short on the way; perhaps I shall be for some good souls a cause of scandal? Finally, being what I am, is it right for me to aspire to anything at all? O my daughters, what a lot of souls there must be to whom the demon brings great losses by thoughts of this kind! They take for humility what I have just said, and many other similar things. . . . This is why I say, my daughters, that, if we wish to learn true humility we must fix our eyes on Jesus Christ, the sovereign good of our souls, and on his saints" (*The Interior Castle, I, 2*). Now, if scruples like these — which

81

are actually pieces of foolishness — are current coin, it is because the very conception of humility has become superficial; only individualistic sentimentalism can give rise to finicalness of this sort on the spiritual plane, and the true remedy would be to purify the idea of humility by bringing it back to its profound meaning, which implies above all a sound knowledge of the nature of things. If humility is subject to so many contortions of the mind, and if the demon has at his disposal so many doors to slip through and take on the appearance of virtue, the reason obviously lies in the sentimental and individualistic corruption of humility itself; in a word, the whole chaos of these entirely artificial difficulties and these almost inextricable psychological subtleties, is due to the abolition — which in its fashion also smacks of pride — of the intelligence. Man no longer "knows" that, metaphysically, he is nothing; he must therefore always be reminding himself, with much effort and sighing, that he is base, unworthy and ungrateful; something that he has difficulty believing in his heart of hearts. It is not sufficiently realized that the devil is not merely in "evil" properly so called, but also, although indirectly, in the insipid exaggeration with which one surrounds the "good," as if to make it suffocating and improbable; whence a pendulum-like play between an "evil" considered as being absolute and endowed with arbitrary contours, and a "good" detached from truth and compromised by the unintelligence of the sentimentalism which accompanies it. Be that as it may, this play of the pendulum between an "evil" made positive and a "good" made improbable and almost inaccessible, cannot be displeasing to the demon, for he has every interest in contributing to a quasi-insoluble alternative which takes possession of the mind, and to an exaggeration which, basically, does wrong to God.[1]

---

1. An example of a healthy attitude is the following meditation of Saint Ignatius of Loyola, in which — instead of abasing himself in an unintelli-

In the same order of ideas, to search after sins denotes a rather outward perspective for, if man is a sinner, it is not in this superficial and quantitative way that he can free himself from his nature. The sound attitude, on this plane, comes down to this: to do what is prescribed, to abstain from what is forbidden, to strive towards the three fundamental virtues from which all others derive, namely humility, charity and veracity. On this basis, our mind can concentrate on God, who will Himself undertake to transform our purely symbolical virtue into an effective and supernatural virtue; for good can come only from Him. Every other attitude is contradictory and unsound; the exaggeration of sin is not possible without individualism; to everywhere and always look for sin is to cultivate it, whereas the aim of spirituality is to transcend the human, not to magnify it. "Be ye therefore perfect, even as your Father which is in heaven is perfect," said Christ; now the perfection of God is a blessed one, which means that the perfection of man must also have an aspect of serenity and peace, which the contemplation of truth confers. It is true that man is free will; but freedom comes from the intelligence, and it is intelligence that characterizes man in the first place.

gible sentiment of gratitude or culpability — he relies, with intelligence, on the nature of things: ". . . I will consider God present in all creatures. He is in the elements, giving them being; in plants, giving them vegetation; in animals, giving them feeling; in men, giving them intelligence; He is in myself in these different manners, giving me at one and the same time being, life, feeling and intelligence. He has done more: He has made of me his temple; and, to this end, He has created me in the likeness and image of his Divine Majesty. . . . I will consider God acting and working for me in all created objects, since He is in fact in the heavens, in the elements, in plants, in fruits, in animals, etc. as an agent, giving to them and conserving for them being, vegetation, feeling, etc. . . . Then, considering seriously my own self, I will ask myself: what do reason and justice oblige me on my part to offer and to give to His Divine Majesty, and that is, all the things that are mine, and myself with them . . ." *(Spiritual Exercises).*

Saint John's doctrine is that of emptiness or obscurity according to faith, hope and charity: emptiness of understanding, memory and will. This conception of hope and charity is universal, but not that of faith: for here emptiness should be, not the negation of pure intelligence, but the negation of the mental element and of formal thought; in other words, instead of comprehension being extinguished before dogma, it is the mental element that has to be extinguished, not before dogma, but before pure intellection, before direct and supra-formal intellective vision. This is obvious, for if love is emptiness of the will, and hope emptiness of the memory, then faith must logically be emptiness of a faculty situated on the same level, namely the mind or reason; faith cannot be emptiness of a faculty incomparably more eminent — because transcending the individual — than will and memory, and above all, it cannot sacrifice the greater for the less, otherwise one could also demand the "emptiness of virtue" by emptying virtue of its contents.

When Saint John of the Cross says that "the soul is not united to God, here below, either through understanding, or through enjoying, or through imagining," one should be entitled, in the case of the first of these three faculties, to read: "through thinking"; and when it is said that "Faith despoils understanding and by its night prevents it from comprehending," one would like to read: "it prevents it from reasoning." One cannot put pure intelligence — which is "something of God" — on the same plane as the strictly individual faculties.

If Saint Paul says that "Faith is the substance of the things which one hopes, a convincing proof of those things which one does not see," this does not of itself mean — though it may do so inclusively and accidentally — what the Spanish Doctor means: "Although the reason adheres absolutely to these things with firmness, they do not disclose themselves to the intelligence, for if they did so, Faith would no longer exist." The most perfect theoretical knowledge cannot abolish existential ignorance; the proof of this is that it does not suffice to have this knowledge in order to behave as if one saw God; on the other hand, metaphysical knowledge is the unquestionable key for the realization of Truth; intellection, by itself, already has the power to purify the heart, so that many of the more or less hazardous complications of individualistic asceticism become superfluous. The difference between faith as belief and faith as gnosis consists in this: that the obscurity of faith, in the ordinary believer, is in the intelligence, whereas in the metaphysician it is in the will, in the participation of his being: the seat of faith is then the heart, not the mind, and the obscurity comes from our state of individuation, not from a congenital unintelligence. The faith of the sage — or of the "gnostic" — has two veils: the body and the ego; they veil, not the intellect, but ontological consciousness. Wisdom, however, comprises degrees.

It would be altogether illogical and disproportionate to ask oneself how the limitations of mystical individualism can accord with sanctity and the most obvious signs of divine grace, ecstasies, levitations and other such phenomena, for religious genius and heroicalness of virtues furnish a sufficient explanation both for the miracle of sanctity and for the miracles of the saints. The scope of the intelligence is an entirely different question: it is only too clear that one cannot say, from a Catholic point view any more than from any other traditional point of view, that heroicalness of virtues and miracles suffice to prove the universal value of a doctrine, otherwise Catholicism for example would have to accept, not only Palamitic theology on account of such saints as Seraphim of Sarow, but even the Asiatic doctrines on account of the unquestionable sanctity of certain of their representatives; one cannot therefore cite, as a criterion of value or of intellectual perfection of the Johnian and Theresian doctrines, the sanctity of their authors, although this sanctity is a guarantee of intrinsic orthodoxy, and even more than that. This is to say that all spiritual paths tend towards Union; it is therefore normal that sanctity as such may comprise "states" and "stations" transcending the possible narrowness of its point of departure or of its initial form; if the aim is Union,[2] this has to be able to manifest itself on the way. In this regard let us again quote Saint Theresa of Avila: "What distinguishes this abode is, as I have said, the almost continual absence of dryness; in it the soul is free from the inward troubles which it experiences from time to time in all other abodes and it nearly always enjoys the purest calm. Far from fearing that the demon can counterfeit so sublime a grace, it remains perfectly assured that God is the author of it; firstly, as has been said, because the senses and the faculties have no part in it, and also because Our Lord, in revealing himself to the soul, has put it with him in a place, which, to my mind, the demon would not dare to enter, and to which moreover the sovereign Master forbids him access. . . . There, our Lord favors the soul and illumines it amidst a peace so profound and of such great silence that it reminds me of the construction of the temple of Solomon, where no sound was to be heard."

2. It is true that Union comprises modes and degrees, but here it is a question of "Union as such" and not of "such and such a Union."

Concerning the Principle
of Sacrifice

Man is as if suspended between Heaven and Earth, or between the Divine Principle and universal Manifestation, so that his destiny is to live in two dimensions: on the one hand, he has the right existentially to experience the gifts of nature without which the earthly human condition would have no positive content; but on the other hand, his spiritual duty is to renounce excess, failing which he would lose his relationship with the heavenly dimension and consequently his salvation. In other words, man may and must be at once "horizontal" and "vertical"; the resulting antinomy is the ransom of the human state, doorway to blessed immortality.

Therefore, contrary to an exclusively ascetical idealism for which the principle of sacrifice alone is spiritually efficacious, the celestial dimension is also to be found in the nobleness and depth of our way of perceiving and assimilating positive phenomena; this perspective finds its justification in the metaphysical transparency of symbols and the mystery of Immanence, and no less so in the fundamental deiformity of the human spirit. But being on Earth, we cannot step out of the limitations of the earthly condition: if it is true that the world manifests Heaven, on the other hand it moves away from it; we cannot escape this ambiguity of creation.

*

*   *

In practice, the principle of sacrifice is this: after the harvest, there is much wheat from which to make bread, but care is taken so as not to make use of all the grain; for one has to be able to sow the field for the next harvest. This sacrifice made by the sower is deeply symbolical: without it, a richness that ought to be renewed would be exhausted; in wanting everything at once, one would be deprived of one's daily bread. Thus it is that life is woven of gifts and sacrifices; only that is enduring which knows how to die in order to be reborn. Whence those "stations of rest" that are the Sabbath, Sunday, Friday among the Moslems, and also, in accordance with a more widely spaced rhythm, the fallow and Ramadan; in nature, night and winter are analogous phenomena. In conjugal life, this principle is a *conditio sine qua non* of stability, hence of happiness; it is necessary to be sober out of respect for beings and things, and this is what the sense of the sacred requires a priori.

Quite evidently, the equilibrium of social as well as individual life is inconceivable without the presence of a regulating sacrificial element; if man fails to pay the tribute he owes nature, then nature will have it paid. Illness and famine, and the other calamities issuing from Pandora's box, did not enter the earthly economy until after the sin of Eve and Adam — Biblically speaking — which was the first disequilibrium, and so to speak the first crime against nature, in itself patient and generous.

According to a mystical German saying, "he who dies before he dies does not die when he dies"; this is the very definition of the sacrificial principle. Life well-lived is paved with acts of renunciation; in order to live in accordance with truth and beauty it is necessary to know how to die. Thus it is that the "Remembrance of God" is a kind of death that day by day interrupts the blind flux of life: without these pauses, the flow of our temporal existence strays and is squandered; with them, it remains faithful to its vocation and is always recreated anew, supernaturally and in the direction of Immortality. In other words, prayer is a death only in relation to our "horizontal" existence and not in itself; it is privative, hence sacrificial, from the standpoint of Manifestation which it denies, and not from the standpoint of the Principle which it affirms.

A doctrinal specification is called for here, for it could be objected that Eternal Life also pertains to Manifestation and consequently is not dispensed from the sacrificial regimen; now this life is celestial, not terrestrial, and thus it can comprise blessed silences — comparable to mild nights on earth — but not privations properly so called. In Heaven, the antinomies of cosmic manifestation are as it were transfigured by God's proximity; it is the whole difference between death and sleep, or between *pralaya,* the cosmic dissolution, and the "night of *Brahmā,*" God's "rest" between two creations of a world. There can be no perfect symmetry between the celestial and terrestrial orders; the fact that the possibilities of the first order are reflected in the second could not mean that the privative or negative possibilities of the latter must be found in the former. The cause of this asymmetry lies in the incommensurability between the world and God; or let us say: in the absolute transcendence of the Supreme Principle, which, from the purely metaphysical[1] point of view, is the only Reality. *Ātmā* can be envisaged without *Māyā,* but there is no *Māyā* without *Ātmā.*[2]

1. As the Sufis say: "The doctrine of Unity is unique." Strictly speaking, gnosis is not a point of view.
2. It cannot validly be objected that the celestial order, and even the personal God, are also situated in *Māyā* and that consequently they pertain to Relativity; for *Māyā* at its summit reflects the incommensurability between the Absolute and the relative, whence the perfectly plausible notion of the "relatively absolute"; and it goes without saying that the "absolutely relative" cannot exist.

*

* *

The sacrificial instinct, which on the whole coincides with the sense of measure, enters into the very definition of nobleness: the noble man is one who controls himself and who loves to control himself; the sense not only of reality, but also of beauty demands that discipline which is self-mastery. Moreover, the impious man can never be altogether noble, whereas piety necessarily gives rise to nobility, no matter what the social milieu; the pious man is noble because truth is noble.

To say piety is to say religion; it is indeed religion that offers to the individual and to society the sacrificial or moral framework without which they cannot subsist in the long run; in this respect, religion has so to speak an ecological function. It cannot be objected that religious moral codes are different and even divergent, for each one is realistic in accordance with its own perspective; each comprises disciplines, equilibratory regulations, sacrifices, and thereby allows one to live with fewer risks with regard to destiny, if one may express oneself thus without being presumptuous.

However, in the case of traditions whose origins are lost in the night of time, this regulative function of religion was not able to prevent abuses or even perversions arising either through excess of zeal or, on the contrary, through lack of vigilance. In civilizations extending over thousands of years, the possible effects of decadence are difficult to foresee — and to prevent — in the absence of sufficient dogmatic precautions. The historical religions wished to avoid these pitfalls, and they managed to do so to a fairly large extent, without however being able to change human nature.[3] Be that as it may, the typically modern solution of

3. Obviously, the faults of the Catholic church, such as the rupture with Byzantium and later the sale of indulgences, cannot be compared

the problem is to abolish the good on account of its possible abuses; in most cases it is readily overlooked that an excess of good is worth more than the absence of it; in reality, all progressivist rebellions are suicides.

In the Latin Church, the sacrificial element has given rise to an ostracism, not of marriage, which is needed in view of procreation and for the survival of Christianity, but of sexuality as such. The effect of this has been on the one hand a complex of sin with a repressed and prudish mentality, and on the other hand opposite reactions which have become manifested since the end of the Middle Ages in the erotic worldliness of princely costumes and in an art that was sensual to the point of being a real obsession. Whence the Renaissance and the Baroque with all their opulence, as far removed as possible from the spirit of renunciation. A curious effect of antisexualist Christianity is what may be termed "moral suspicion," which causes the average Christian to be viscerally blocked in regard to the spiritualized sexuality of Easterners, because his imagination does not allow him to conceive of such a possibility.

Let us now change the cultural setting but not the subject: one of the most widespread abuses of the sacrificial perspective is the permanent intertribal war among so-called primitive peoples, and also among the warrior castes of urban civilizations. Of course, if the Red Indians, for example, are almost always on the warpath, it is a priori out of a kind of spiritual as well as ecological realism: as we have remarked in an earlier chapter, the fundamental idea is that without permanent ordeals, society degenerates; this is true for a society of *kshatriyas,* as the Hindus would say, but not for a society of *brāhmanas.*[4] If the great majority of a human

with the deviation of the Babylonian or Aztec paganisms, which seems to have affected the very substance of these religions.

4. Let us recall that the *kshatriya* is the man of action, intelligent but passional, and in any case of noble character, whereas the *brāhmana* is

collectivity were composed of intellectually and spiritually very superior man — who bear sacrifice and victory within themselves — endemic war would not be useful, let alone necessary; but such societies no longer exist, and consequently — as is attested by the *Bhagavad Gītā* — battle between heroes is a good, from the standpoint of character formation as well as of racial hygiene, notwithstanding that continual fights between tribes unquestionably involve abusive elements, in conformity with the general tendency of the "Iron Age."[5]

As for the modern Western world — which increasingly encroaches upon the entire globe — one has to face the fact that it represents the very negation of the sacrificial principle, owing to its unrealistic perfectionism. This lack of realism is the result of the notions of "civilization" and "progress": an absolute perfection is just as impossible here below as is an unlimited improvement; he who wants everything risks losing everything.[6] Not that one should want to remain imperfect, but perfection has to be envisaged in all of its aspects and the hierarchy of values taken into account; nothing stable can be realized outwardly without the concurrence of the inward dimension which has priority and which, precisely, demands the intervention of the "celestial void" that is sacrifice.

essentially the intellective and contemplative, hence also the man who is peaceable without being weak.

5. Originally, wars between the Red Indians — according to a historian — were only "somewhat bloody tournaments." The same remark can be applied to the Bedouins, whose warlike customs were moreover notably generous: it was forbidden to touch a woman in the enemy camp, and the indispensable implements for surviving in the desert were not to be taken away.

6. "Liberty, equality, fraternity": values that on the one hand are relative and on the other hand have their foundation in eschatology; by separating them from this basis and by attributing an absolute character to them, one inevitably falls into their opposites.

*

* *

Undoubtedly, the sacrificial principle as such is a negative thing, but since it is rooted in the Sovereign Good and has its sufficient reason therein, it necessarily comprises an element of happiness: "I am black but beautiful," says the Song of Songs; and also: "Thou art all fair, my love; there is no spot in thee."

In any case, man must not allow his renunciation to give rise to a "zeal of bitterness that leads to hell"; the Sermon on the Mount insists upon this: "Moreover, when ye fast, be not, as the hypocrites, of a sad countenance . . . But thou, when thou fastest, anoint thine head, and wash thy face . . ." In other words, sacrifice ought to include an element of beauty or — what amounts to the same thing — an element of love: "Though I speak with the tongues of men and of angels, and have not charity, I am become as sounding brass, or a tinkling cymbal"; that is, a noise without content, or a discourse without message.

The sacrificial attitude comprises two positive compensatory elements, namely virtue and grace; the latter coming from God, and the former from ourselves. On the one hand, man must realize the attitudes of resignation and trust, or of serenity and certitude; on the other hand, God grants graces when He wills; Saint Mary Magdalene, who spent her days in solitude and prayer — completely naked, according to early images[7] — was every day lifted up to Paradise by angels.

*

* *

A question that may arise is that of knowing whether the distinction between the "flesh" and the "spirit" is the

---

7. Which symbolizes negatively poverty before God, and positively, man's deiformity.

equivalent of that between "sensible consolations" and the sacrificial principle; this is true within the limits of a certain perspective in itself legitimate, but not beyond; for on the one hand the "spirit" can ennoble and deepen the "flesh" which is then situated on the side of the "spirit," and on the other hand, the "flesh" can impoverish and adulterate the "spirit" which is then situated on the side of the "flesh."[8] By "flesh," we mean here all that is natural, not supernatural, and by "spirit," that which leads to God in a direct manner, hence by definition; but this does not mean that a natural thing could not bring one closer to God in an indirect and conditional manner, as is notably the case with sacred art; with all due deferance to those monks who consider that a monastery chapel ought to be totally empty and poor, which may be right vocationally and for themselves, but not from the viewpoint of the nature of things. In a word: all that in itself does not lead to God and can even lead away from Him is of the "flesh"; all that in fact brings us closer to God is of the "spirit."[9]

Taking into account the fact that according to a — rightly or wrongly — universally recognized terminology, the word "philosophy" designates all that extrinsically pertains to thought, we would say that there is a philosophy according to the "spirit," which is founded on pure intellection — possibly actualized by a particular sacred Text — and a philosophy according to the "flesh," which is founded on individual reasoning in the absence of sufficient data and of any supernatural intuition; the first being the *philosophia*

8. In a relative sense and without wishing to underestimate Aristotle's merits, it could be said that this philosopher "carnalized" the "divine" Plato by putting forward a metaphysics turned towards earthly experience. However, the Stagirite cannot be accused, as regards the essential, of any false idea; limitation is not error.

9. Especially beauty perceived by a noble man, that is: whose soul is beautiful, precisely. As Socrates said: "If there be something other than absolute Beauty, then that something can be beautiful to the extent that it partakes of absolute Beauty" (Plato: *Phaedo*).

perennis, and the second, the ancient Protagorism as well as the rationalist thought of the moderns.[10]

We have gone into these details here because for some only the principle of sacrifice — along with Revelation and Grace — is on the side of the "spirit"; they are right in the sense that to accept sincerely the transcendent truth — whose nature is to annihilate our illusions — is to die a little; but it is also to be reborn and to live, beyond all that the earthly ego could ever imagine.

---

10. Even if it resists being rationalism, which is of no importance and which evokes this line of Shakespeare: "Though this be madness, yet there is method in it."

Dimensions of Prayer

Man must meet God with all that he is, for God is the Being of all; that is the meaning of the Biblical injunction to love God "with all our strength." Now, one of the dimensions that characterizes man de facto is that he lives towards the exterior and, in addition, that he tends towards pleasures; this is his outwardness and his concupiscence. He must renounce them in the face of God, for firstly, God is present in us, and secondly, man must be able to find pleasure within himself and independently of sensorial phenomena.

But everything that brings one closer to God partakes of His beatitude for that very reason; to rise, by praying, above the images and noise of the soul, is a liberation through the Divine Void and Infinitude; it is the station of serenity.

It is true that outward phenomena, by their nobleness and their symbolism — their participation in the celestial Archetypes — can have an interiorizing virtue, and everything can be good in its season; nevertheless detachment has to be realized, otherwise man does not have the right to legitimate outwardness, and otherwise he would fall into a seductive outwardness and a concupiscence which are mortal for the soul. Just as the Creator by His transcendence is independent of the creation, so man must be independent of the world in view of God. This is the free will that is man's endowment; only man is capable of resisting his instincts and desires. *Vacare Deo.*

97

*

* *

Another of man's endowments is reasoning thought and speech; this dimension must in consequence be actualized during that encounter with God which is prayer. Man is saved not only by abstaining from evil, he also, and a fortiori, is saved by accomplishing good; now the best of works is that which has God as its object and our heart as its agent, and this is the "remembrance of God."

The essence of prayer is faith, hence certitude; man manifests it precisely by speech, or appeals, addressed to the Sovereign Good. Prayer, or invocation, equals certitude of God and of our spiritual vocation.

Action is valid according to its intention; it is obvious that in prayer there must be no intention tainted with ambition of any kind; it must be pure of all worldly vanity, on pain of provoking the Wrath of Heaven.

Wholehearted prayer benefits not only him who accomplishes it, it also radiates around him, and in this respect it is an act of charity.

*

* *

Every man is in search of happiness; this is another dimension of human nature. Now there is no perfect happiness outside God; any earthly happiness has need of Heaven's blessing. Prayer places us in the presence of God Who is pure Beatitude; if we are aware of this, we will find Peace in it. Happy the man who has the sense of the Sacred and who thus opens his heart to this mystery.

*

* *

Another dimension of prayer stems from the fact that on the one hand man is mortal, and that on the other he has an immortal soul; he must pass through death, and above all, he must be concerned with Eternity, which is in God's Hands.

In this context, prayer will be at once an appeal to Mercy and an act of faith and trust.

*

* *

Man's fundamental endowment is an intelligence capable of metaphysical knowledge; consequently, this capacity necessarily determines a dimension of prayer, which then coincides with meditation; its subject is firstly the absolute reality of the Supreme Principle, and then the non-reality — or the relative reality — of the world which manifests It.

However, man must not make use of intentions that surpass his nature; if he is not a metaphysician, he must not believe himself obliged to be one. God loves children just as He loves sages; and He loves the sincerity of the child who knows how to remain a child.

This means that in prayer there are dimensions that are imperative for every man, and others that he may as it were greet from afar; for what matters in this confrontation is not that man be great or small, but that he stand sincerely before God. On the one hand, man is always small before his Creator; on the other hand, there is always greatness in man when he addresses God; and in the final analysis, every quality and every merit belong to the Sovereign Good.

*

* *

We have said that there is a dimension of meditative prayer whose content is the absolute reality of the Principle; and then, correlatively, the non-reality — or the lesser reality — of the world, which manifests It.

But it is not enough to know that *"Brahma* is Reality, the world is appearance"; it is also necessary to know that "the soul is not other than *Brahma."* This second truth reminds

99

us that we are able, if our nature allows it, to tend towards the Supreme Principle not only in intellectual mode, but also in existential mode; which stems from the fact that we possess not only an intelligence capable of objective knowledge, but also the consciousness of the "I," which in principle is capable of subjective union. On the one hand, the ego is separated from the immanent Divinity because it is manifestation, not Principle; on the other hand, it is not other than the Principle inasmuch as the Principle manifests Itself; just as the reflection of the sun in a mirror is not the sun, but is nevertheless "not other than it" inasmuch as the reflection is solar light and nothing else.

Aware of this, man does not cease to stand before God, Who is at once transcendent and immanent; and it is He, and not we, Who decides the scope of our contemplative awareness and the mystery of our spiritual destiny. We know that to know God unitively means that God Himself knows Himself in us; but we cannot know to what extent He intends to realize in us this divine Self-Consciousness; and it is of no importance that we know it or not. We are what we are, and everything is in the hands of Providence.

Part Three

Excerpts from Correspondence*

The Garden

A man sees a beautiful garden, but he knows: he will not always see these flowers and bushes, because one day he will die; and he also knows: the garden will not always be there, because this world will disappear in its turn. And he knows also: this relationship with the beautiful garden is the gift of destiny, because if a man were to find himself in the middle of a desert, he would not see the garden; he sees it only because destiny has put him, man, here and not elsewhere.

But in the innermost region of our soul dwells the Spirit, and in it is contained the garden, as it were, like a seed; and if we love this garden — and how could we not love it since it is of a heavenly beauty? — we would do well to look for it where it has always been and always will be, that is to say in the Spirit; maintain yourself in the Spirit, in your own center, and you will have the garden and in addition all possible gardens. Similarly: in the Spirit there is no death, because here you are immortal; and in the Spirit the relationship between the contemplator and the contemplated is not only a fragile possibility; on the contrary, it is part of the very nature of the Spirit and, like it, it is eternal.

The Spirit is Consciousness and Will: Consciousness of oneself and Will towards oneself. Maintain yourself in the Spirit through Consciousness, and approach the Spirit through the Will or through Love; then neither death nor the end of the world can take away the garden from you nor destroy your vision. Whatever you are in the Spirit now, you will remain so after death; and whatever is yours in the Spirit now, will be yours after death. Before God there is neither being nor ownership except in the Spirit; whatever was outward must become inward and whatever was inward will become outward: look for the garden within yourself, in your indestructible divine Substance, which then will give you a new and imperishable garden.

The Ordeal

There is a moment in life when a man makes the decision to move closer to God; to realize a permanent relationship with his Creator; to become what he should have been — by the fundamental vocation of the human state — ever since the age of reason; in a word, to attain primordial innocence and to enjoy the proximity of the Sovereign Good, whether we call this privilege "Salvation" or "Union."

It is in the nature of things that man be conscious of the happiness that his choice implies and that at the beginning of the Path he be full of enthusiasm; in many cases however, the aspirant is unaware that he will have to go through difficulties he carries within himself and which are aroused and unfolded by the contact with a heavenly element. These lower psychic possibilities — quite evidently incompatible with perfection — must be exhausted and dissolved; it is this that has been variously called the "initiatic ordeal," the "descent into hell," the "temptation of the hero" or the "great holy war." These psychic elements can be either hereditary or personal; furthermore, we can be fully responsible for them or on the contrary be affected by them due to pressure from a given environment; they can take the form of a discouragement, of a doubt, of a revolt, and it is then more important than ever not to listen to the voice of the profane ego, by opening oneself thus to the influence of the demon and embarking on the downward slope of either despair or subversion. Also, the *sine qua non* of spiritual health and of upward movement is a merciless discernment in regard to oneself, beside the fundamental quality which is the fear of God; hence the sense of the sacred, the sense of proportion, and also — it must be understood — the sense of grandeur and of beauty.

According to a Hindu and Buddhist symbolism, the situation of earthly man is that of a turtle swimming in the ocean upon whose surface, somewhere far away, there floats a plank of wood with a knothole in it; now, the turtle is supposed to put its head through that knothole, and it is thus that a man must seek and find the liberating Path; the immensity of the ocean represents the immensity of the universe, of the *samsāra,* of our existential space. "Blessed is the man who has overcome the ordeal!"

Certitudes

I know with certitude that there are phenomena, and that I myself am one of them.

I know with certitude that underlying the phenomena, or beyond them, there is the one Essence, which the phenomena manifest in function of a quality of this Essence, that of Infinitude, hence of Radiation.

I know with certitude that the Essence is good and that all goodness or beauty in phenomena is a manifestation thereof.

I know with certitude that the phenomena will return to the Essence, from which they are not really separate, since at bottom It alone is; that they will return to the Essence because apart from It nothing is absolute nor in consequence eternal; that Manifestation is necessarily subject to a rhythm, as it is necessarily subject to a hierarchy.

I know with certitude that the soul is immortal, for its indestructibility results from the very nature of the intelligence.

I know with certitude that underlying the diverse consciousnesses there is but one sole Subject: the Self at once transcendent and immanent, accessible through the Intellect, seat or organ of the religion of the Heart; for the diverse consciousnesses exclude and contradict one another, whereas the Self includes all and is contradicted by none.

I know with certitude that the Essence, God, affirms Itself with regard to phenomena, the world, as Power of Attraction and Will of Equilibrium; that we are made in order to follow vertically this Attraction, and that we cannot do this unless we conform, horizontally, to the Equilibrium manifested by sacred and natural Laws.

On Holiness

Holiness is the sleep of the ego and the wake of the immortal soul. The moving surface of our being must sleep and must therefore withdraw from images and instincts, whereas the depths of our being must be awake in the consciousness of the Divine, thus lighting up, like a motionless flame, the silence of the holy sleep.

This sleep implies essentially repose in the Divine Will, and this repose is the return to the root of our existence, of our being as willed by God. Repose in Being is the deepest conformity to the Will of Heaven; now, this Being is both Consciousness and Goodness, and it is only through consciousness of the Absolute and through goodness — or through beauty of soul — that we can attain to Being, *Deo volente*.

The habitual dream of man lives on the past and the future, the heart is as it were chained to the past and at the same time swept away by the future, instead of reposing in the "Now" of Being; in this Eternal Present that is Peace, Consciousness of Self and Radiation of Life.

Love of God

Love of God is the happiness we experience in a state of soul that comes from God and leads to God; in other words, it is the happiness that God confers upon us through particular aspects of His Nature, and the attraction that He consequently exerts on us.

On the one hand, "our Father who art in Heaven"; but on the other hand, "the Kingdom of God is within you." This is to say that these states of soul, or these modes of love or happiness, are basically of two kinds, according to whether they pertain to "Heaven," which is above us and above the din of the world, or to the inward "Kingdom," which is within ourselves and in the depths of our heart. The first happiness is that of Infinitude and Freedom; the second, that of Centrality and Security; or again, the first is the happiness of Serenity, and the second that of Certitude.

Gratitude

There are the archetypes, which are eternal since they are contained in the divine Intellect, and there are their terrestrial reflections, which are temporal and ephemeral since they are projected into the moving substance that is relativity or contingency. Wisdom consists not only in becoming detached from the reflections, but also in knowing and feeling that the archetypes are to be found within ourselves and are accessible in the depths of our hearts; we possess what we love to the extent that what we love is worthy of being loved.

Instead of having his gaze always fixed on the imperfections of the world and the vicissitudes of life, man should never lose sight of the good fortune of being born in the human state, which is the road leading to Heaven. One praises God, not only because He is the Sovereign Good, but also because He has given us birth at the gate of Paradise; this means that man is made for all that leads there: for the Truth, for the Path and for Virtue.

Weakness and Strength

Weakness is the habitual conviction of being weak; to be weak is to be unaware that every man has access to strength, to all the strength there is. Strength is not a privilege of the strong, it is a potentiality of every man; the problem is to find access to this strength.

To be weak is to be passively subject to duration; to be strong is to be actively free in the instant, in the Eternal Present.

To be weak is to give way to pressures, and one gives way to pressures because one does not see the effects in the causes. Sin is a cause, punishment is its concordant effect. Man is weak because he lacks faith; his faith is abstract, hypocritical and inoperative; he believes in Heaven and in Hell, but he behaves as if he did not believe in them. Now we must flee from evil as we would flee from a fire we see rushing towards us, and we must attach ourselves to the good as we would attach ourselves to an oasis we see in the midst of a desert.

Complementarities

The virtue of resignation, or patience or detachment, is perfect only with the help of the virtue of trust, or hope or faith, which adds to it an element of active mildness; conversely and with all the more reason, the virtue of trust is perfect only with the help of the virtue of resignation, which adds to it an element of passive rigor; every virtue implying, moreover, the graces of certitude and serenity.

And likewise: the virtue of zeal, or fervor or initiative, is perfect only with the help of the virtue of contentment, or of recollection or tranquility, which adds to it an element of passive mildness; conversely and a fortiori, the virtue of contentment is perfect only with the help of the virtue of zeal, which adds to it an element of active rigor; perfection lies in the equilibrium of complementary opposites.

And likewise again: the virtue of humility, or sincerity or self-effacement, or the awareness of our limitations, must be accompanied by the virtue of dignity, of inwardness, of existential consciousness of the Divine Majesty, for man is "made in the image of God"; conversely, the virtue of dignity must be founded on the virtue of humility, for "God alone is good."

Lastly, the virtue of charity, or generosity, must be accompanied by the virtue of justice, thus by a sense of duties and rights, for "there is no right superior to that of truth"; conversely, the rigor of justice will be compensated by the mildness of charity, for "love thy neighbor as thyself." "Verily, My Mercy hath precedence over My Wrath."

To Earn One's Salvation

Being saved, and bringing others to be saved; there lies our whole vocation. It has been likewise said that the good tends by its nature to communicate itself.

For salvation, two things are needed before all else: Truth and Faith. Knowing something, and believing in something; that is to say: Knowledge of the Truth and union with the Truth.

And so also for Faith two things are needful, and they concern our will: namely, an activity and an abstention. Doing what is in conformity with Truth and what gives life and depth to Faith; abstaining from what is contrary to Truth and from what is harmful to Faith.

To be able to realize this throughout the whole of life, the soul has need of two virtues: Patience and Trust. Enduring for God, and rejoicing in God.

Everything is there. We cannot do anything better either for ourselves or for our fellows; one would almost like to say: he who does not wish to be saved for his own sake, let him at least seek salvation for the love of others. For the good has a liberating radiance, whether we know it or not, and whether we have an outward vocation or not; not everyone has to teach, but everyone must be holy. In any case: the obtaining of salvation is accompanied by the consciousness that it benefits others also.

The symbolism of the lamp teaches us the relationship between Truth and Faith: the light is Truth, and the oil is Faith. Oil already somehow possesses luminosity in its own substance; this is inward Truth, inborn in us and inherent in our deepest nature. Or again: water is Truth, and wine is Faith.

The Sense of the Sacred

The sense of the sacred, or the love of sacred things — whether of symbols or of modes of Divine Presence — is a *conditio sine qua non* of Knowledge, which engages not only our intelligence, but all the powers of our soul; for the Divine All demands the human all.

The sense of the sacred, which is none other than the quasi-natural predisposition to the love of God and the sensitivity to theophanic manifestations or to celestial perfumes — this sense of the sacred implies essentially the sense of beauty and the tendency toward virtue; beauty is outward virtue as it were, and virtue, inward beauty. It also implies the sense of the metaphysical transparency of phenomena, that is, the capacity of grasping the principial within the manifested, the uncreated within the created; or of perceiving the vertical ray, messenger of the Archetype, independently of the plane of horizontal refraction, which determines the existential degree, but not the divine content.

On Virtue

One must realize the virtues for their own sake, and not in order to make them "mine."

One may be sad because one displeases God, but not because one is not holy while others are.

To understand a virtue is to know how to realize it; to understand a fault is to know how to overcome it. To be sad because one does not know how to overcome a fault shows that one has not understood the nature of the corresponding virtue and that one's aspiration is motivated by egoism. Truth must be given precedence over self-interest.

To have a virtue is above all to be without the fault that is contrary to it, for God created us virtuous. He created us in His image; faults are superimposed. Moreover, it is not we who possess virtue, it is virtue which possesses us.

Vice, like every other privative and malefic phenomenon, is so to speak an irruption of nothingness into existence: it is a negation of Being, but it is ontologically condemned to imitate what it intends to deny, for this "existentialized" naught can do nothing of itself, precisely because it is nothing in itself.

Virtue, for its part, is a message from Being; it is like a reverberation of the Sovereign Good, in which we participate through our nature or through our will, easily or with difficulty, but always by the Grace of He who is.

Treasures

The Orison-Form — and quintessentially the Divine Name — contains God's will to save man.

The Orison-Act — and quintessentially the human heart — contains man's desire to be saved.

Orison contains and communicates all the treasures of the Divine Presence and of human faith.

Where there is Truth, there is Salvation.

Where there is Certitude, there is Peace.

Where there is Prayer, there is Grace.

Where there is Fervor, there is Victory.

It has been said: "Where thy treasure is, there will thy heart be also." May man recognize his treasure in liberating Truth, with his whole heart.

The Ransom of the Self

To say "individual" is to say "destiny." If I am I, I must necessarily live in a given time, at a given moment, in a given world, in a given place; I must live a given experience and a given happiness; I do not have full access to Happiness as such.

The individual is, by definition, suspended between a particular form of happiness and Happiness as such; he can feel what is arbitrary in earthly particularity, but he cannot escape this particularity any more than he can escape his individuality. In this there is a kind of "illogicality" which may disturb him, but he must resign himself to it, and more than that; he must try to mitigate it, or even transcend it, by drawing near to the Archetype, to the celestial and divine In-Itself; not to a particular good, but to the Good as such.

One might object here that in Heaven the individuality subsists, and that in consequence one does not escape the antinomy in question; which is at once true and false. It is true in the sense that paradisal Happiness lived by a given individual is necessarily a particular happiness; but it is false in the sense that every paradisal Happiness is transparent in the direction of God, which is to say that it is so penetrated by Happiness as such that there no longer remains any ambiguity in it. On the one hand "there are many rooms in my Father's Mansions"; on the other hand, Beatitude is one because Salvation is one, and because God is One.

116

Two Visions of Things

It has been said that one must see God in everything; it has also been said that one must see everything in God. The first expression means that in perceiving a positive phenomenon — for it is this category that is in question — man must perceive the divine cause; he must not stop short at the gross appearance; he must see the Principle in manifestation, the archetypal intention in the contingent form. It is necessary to see the essential in things rather than the accidental.

The second expression relates to the perceiving subject, not to the object perceived; it means that man must see things according to the spirit of the Creator, not with the superficial, profane and desacralizing view of the vulgar soul. The noble man feels the need to admire, to venerate, to worship; the vile man on the contrary tends to belittle, even to mock, which is the way the devil sees things; but it is also diabolical to admire what is evil, whereas it is normal and praiseworthy to despise evil as such, for the truth has precedence over everything. The primacy of the true also clearly implies that essential truths have precedence over secondary truths, as the absolute has precedence over the relative. The definition of man according to immortality has precedence over the definition of man according to earthly life.

If on the one hand we must try to realize the ideal starting from the Divine by means of the Truth and the Path, on the other hand we must make that effort starting from the human through our way of looking at that manifestation of God which is the world. "Unto the pure, all things are pure"; but also "Unto the impure, all things are impure." To see the essential in the contingent or in the accidental is to look at things as if we were in God and hence no longer saw anything other than Him; and to see things with an essentializing eye — one that relays the accident to the archetype — is as if God were in us and hence we no longer saw except through Him. And if the modes of the Divine Presence — may God grant us this! — are equivalent to the noble and metaphysically realistic vision of the world and of life, this vision in its turn opens the way towards this liberating Presence; distant, perhaps, yet profoundly inscribed in our nature.

Manifestation and Proof

A proof presupposes: the absence of what is to be proven; the presence of an element that in some way is part of the thing to be proven; an epistemological axiom that renders a proof possible and therefore efficacious. The proof prolongs the thing to be proven, either directly or indirectly: in the first case, the effect is of the same order as the cause; in the second case, the effect is of another order, which means that the causality is "vertical" and not "horizontal." Be that as it may, the proof is by definition a direct or indirect manifestation of the thing to be proven.

There are agnostics who deny even the necessity of a cause; now in the absence of this axiom, which pertains to the nature of the intelligence, no proof is possible.

It is an essential principle that the organ of knowledge must be proportioned to the thing to be known! For sceptics, this requirement is a *petitio principii,* since for them the question of epistemological qualification does not arise; and what transcends sensorial knowledge and the empirical order does not exist in their opinion.

To ask for a proof of the Absolute is absurd for two reasons, one objective and the other subjective: firstly, the Absolute cannot enter the phenomenal order, hence there is no common measure; secondly, if our intelligence is qualified for conceiving the Absolute, it will not require proofs on the plane of contingency or of relativity. However, these proofs necessarily exist because everything is a manifestation of the Absolute; but only sound intelligences, capable of intellectual intuition because inspired by the Absolute Itself, will attain to them. "The soul is not other than *Brahma.*"

To say proof is to say direct or indirect manifestation; consequently, the existence of things proves the Absolute since existence manifests It.

To say Absolute is to say Infinite; and what manifests the Infinite, and therefore proves It, is the indefinite diversity of things and the illimitation of their containers, which are the existential categories, such as space, time, form, number, matter, energy.

And similarly: to say Absolute or Infinite, is to say radiating Good, Goodness, Beauty, Beatitude; and what manifests, and thereby proves, this hypostatic dimension is the whole of the positive qualities of things, including the faculties of creatures; and also, in an indirect and *a contrario* fashion, imperfections or flaws — through privation or through excess — which manifest the Good without wishing to, by denying and falsifying It. Now to deny the Good is to manifest It through contrast; the absolute Good is beyond all possible opposition.

This is not to say that the Real has need of any proof, nor that the Intellect has need of proof for its certitude; but the proof is there, and in its way it is a presence of God, with all that this demands of us, and with all that it offers us.

Sufic Onomatology

"The First" *(Al-Awwal):* the Supreme Principle insofar as It is "before" Manifestation, and insofar as its Infinitude "desires" its Radiation. Mystery of the Origin, of the primordial Perfection.

"The Last" *(Al-Ākhir):* The Principle insofar as It is "after" Manifestation, and insofar as its Absoluteness "desires" its Unicity. Mystery of the final Good, of eternal Peace.

"The Outward" *(Azh-Zhāhir):* the Principle insofar as It manifests Itself through and in the World; from this derives the perspective of analogy. Mystery of universal Manifestation; of Symbolism.

"The Inward" *(Al-Bāṭin):* the Principle insofar as It remains hidden behind the appearances of Manifestation; from this derives the perspective of abstraction. Mystery of Immanence as well as of Transcendence.

"God" *(Allāh):* the Principle insofar as It includes all of its possible aspects. Mystery of Divinity.

"The One" *(Al-Aḥad):* the Principle insofar as It is One in Itself. Mystery of intrinsic Unity.

"The Unique" *(Al-Wāḥid):* the Principle insofar as It is One in relation to Manifestation. Mystery of extrinsic Unity.

"The Impenetrable" *(Aṣ-Ṣamad):* the Principle insofar as nothing can be added to It, given that It contains everything; there is nothing that It does not already possess, thus nothing can enter into It. Mystery of Exclusivity.

"He" *(Huwa):* the Principle insofar as It is Itself; the Essence beyond the Qualities. Mystery of Ipseity, of Essentiality, of Aseity.

"There is no divinity save the sole Divinity" *(Lā ilāha illā 'Llāh):* the Principle insofar as It excludes and annuls the illusory World, while at the same time affirming the unique and supreme Reality. Mystery of Negation and of Affirmation; of Reality.

"The Clement" *(Ar-Raḥmān)*: the Principle insofar as it is in its nature to wish to communicate its Goodness, its Beauty, its Beatitude; insofar as It is the Sovereign Good "before" the creation of the World. Mystery of intrinsic Goodness.

"The Merciful" *(Ar-Raḥīm)*: the Principle insofar as It manifests its Goodness "after" the creation of the World and within it. Mystery of extrinsic Goodness.

Existence and Divine Presence

When by destiny we encounter an earthly reality that we can love, it seems to say to us: being a form, I am necessarily "this particular form"; I cannot be another form than the one I am, nor all forms at once; and being "this particular form," I cannot be "form as such," for then I would be a heavenly archetype and thereby an unperceivable reality. Moreover: I am inevitably — in duration — one event and not another; in a word, being a possibility, I must be a particular possibility which excludes everything that is not itself.

And the event-form could also say to us: in space, I must be "here," where I am in fact, capable of being neither elsewhere nor everywhere; in time, I must be "now," capable of being neither at another moment nor always.

The heavenly regions, which are close to God, exclude ipso facto all privative elements; but they cannot exclude the existential limitations of form and event. In Heaven there reigns the climate of the archetypes; now, the only phenomena which possess an archetype are the positive ones — those that manifest a Divine Quality or Function — and not the negative or privative ones, which derive, not from Being, but from an absence of Being, metaphysically speaking; evil as such cannot have a heavenly or divine prototype, but it does have one as regards existential or functional qualities; in this case there is no longer a question of evil, precisely, for Heaven belongs to the Kingdom of the Sovereign Good; *adveniat Regnum tuum*.

In a certain sense, there are nothing but archetypes in Paradise, since evil is absent there, which implies that in the archetypes there is a hierarchy: a man purified of his defects coincides indeed with his own primordial model, but he may realize other modes of human perfection as well — for there are also functions and ethnic characteristics — and a fortiori the absolute archetype, which is "man as such" and not merely "such and such a man." Now, man "made in the image of God" is the cosmic mirror which God has projected in order to reflect Himself in it in the mode of relativity, according to the demands of the illimitation of Divine Possibility. It is in this sense that for the Sufis the World is "Universal Man"; the microcosm and the macrocosm meet in a single mystery.

In Heaven there is a factor of synthesis and liberation unknown to the earthly world, and that is the Divine Presence; this Presence is not really absent from the world, but in the world it is not perceivable, whereas in Paradise it is; it pervades all things and thereby unites them. It is thus that in the Divine Proximity existential limitations are compensated by an illimitation everywhere present; Existence divides and excludes, the Divine Presence unites and includes.

Blessed the man who bears in his earthly heart the foreshadowings of his heavenly ambience.

The Two Great Moments

There are two moments in life which are everything, and these are the present moment, when we are free to choose what we wish to be, and the moment of death, when we have no longer any choice and when the decision belongs to God.

If the present moment is good, death will be good; if we are now with God — in this present which ceaselessly renews itself but which remains always this one and only moment of actuality — God will be with us at the moment of our death.

The remembrance of God is a death in life; it will be a life in death.

Analogously: if we enter into God, God will enter into us.

If we dwell in that center which is His Name, God will dwell in that center which is our heart. In the whole extent of the world, there is nothing else than this reciprocity: for the center is everywhere, just as the present is always.

Between the present moment, when we remember God, and death, when God will remember us, there is the rest of life, the duration which extends from the present moment to the last moment; but duration is merely a succession of present moments, for we live always "now"; it is thus, concretely and operatively speaking, always the same blessed instant in which we are free to remember God and to find our happiness in this Remembrance.

We are not free to escape from death, but we are free to choose God, in this present moment which sums up every possible moment. It is true that God alone is absolutely free; but our freedom is nonetheless real at its own level — otherwise the word would not exist — since it manifests the Freedom of God and therefore participates in it. In God, we are as free as we can be, and to the extent that God reintegrates us into His Infinite Freedom.

125

BY THE SAME AUTHOR

The Transcendent Unity of Religions, *1953*
Revised Edition, *1975, 1984, The Theosophical Publishing House, 1993*

Spiritual Perspectives and Human Facts, *1954, 1969*
New Translation, *Perennial Books, 1987*

Gnosis: Divine Wisdom, *1959, 1978, Perennial Books 1990*

Stations of Wisdom, *1961, 1980*
Revised Translation, *World Wisdom Books, 1995*

Understanding Islam, *1963, 1965, 1972, 1976, 1979, 1981, 1986, 1989*
Revised Translation, *World Wisdom Books, 1994*

Light on the Ancient Worlds, *1966, World Wisdom Books, 1984*

In the Tracks of Buddhism, *1968, 1989*
New Translation, Treasures of Buddhism, *World Wisdom Books, 1993*

Logic and Transcendence, *1975, Perennial Books, 1984*

Esoterism as Principle and as Way, *Perennial Books, 1981, 1990*

Castes and Races, *Perennial Books, 1959, 1982*

Sufism: Veil and Quintessence, *World Wisdom Books, 1981*

From the Divine to the Human, *World Wisdom Books, 1982*

Christianity/Islam, *World Wisdom Books, 1985*

The Essential Writings of Frithjof Schuon (S. H. Nasr, Ed.)
1986, Element, 1991

Survey of Metaphysics & Esoterism, *World Wisdom Books, 1986*

In the Face of the Absolute, *World Wisdom Books, 1989, 1994*

The Feathered Sun: Plains Indians in Art & Philosophy,
World Wisdom Books, 1990

To Have a Center, *World Wisdom Books, 1990*

Roots of the Human Condition, *World Wisdom Books, 1991*

Images of Primordial & Mystic Beauty: Paintings by Frithjof Schuon,
Abodes, 1992

Echoes of Perennial Wisdom, *World Wisdom Books, 1992*

The Play of Masks, *World Wisdom Books, 1992*

Road to the Heart, *World Wisdom Books, in preparation*